ANGIE HAMMOND

UNPACKING

A life unpacked, unedited and mostly unashamed

Unpacking:
A life unpacked, unedited and mostly unashamed

Author: Angie Hammond
Graphic Design: Melissa Corrêa
ISBN 978-0-6485196-0-7
First Edition 2019
Printed in Australia

Copyright © 2019 by Angie Hammond
All rights reserved. This book or any portion thereof may not be reproduced or used in any manner whatsoever without the express written permission of the publisher except for the use of brief quotations in a book review.

This book is a work of nonfiction, therefore certain names and identifying characteristics have been changed to protect the people in the stories. This book is told from the authors perspective based on her memories and nothing else.

Credit goes to Elizabeth Gilbert - Big Magic as I mention the book on page 17;
Acknowledgement to Crowded House, Distant Sun as the song's lyrics are mentioned on page 64.

Dedicated to My Hubby Kev
For your trust, encouragement and patience

Acknowledgements

I'd like to pay special thanks to a number of people who made my journey through life what it is today.

First up – My Mum and Dad. Without their guidance and support for me to be exactly whom I wanted to be without trying to shape or mold me I would not be the person I am today. My Dad taught me to get on with the job, not to give in. My mum taught me to be strong, independent and resilient.

To KJ for her steadfast honest and sometimes brutal advice has helped me to stay true to who I am. For her shoulder, ear and wise words I am forever grateful, you are a true friend.

To Sally who walked me through the pain of the last few years – thank you. Being there when I needed a beer, a chat, a coffee or some impartial advice – you have been a rock to me and will always be one of my closest mates.

To Malin – Saturdays are now awesome when we go out on our long rides. Thanks Chook – you rock.

To my children for putting up with me when it felt like I was losing the plot, for your unwavering and unconditional love.. You are my pride and joy. Jake and Zak you are the best things to have ever happened to me and I am so proud of the humans you are evolving into, you will succeed in this world because of your sheer ability to get on with it, understand right from wrong and be polite. You are full of gumption and desire to do well – no matter what the challenge – go get em guys.

To my book mentor Dixie for believing in me. Our weekly conversations have helped me to shape this book to where it is today – I cannot thank you enough.

Lastly but definitely not least to my husband for your ability to forgive me, change yourself and go through your metamorphosis into the beautiful man you are today. We are both works in progress - as we all are, but your resilience, love and persistence with me and us amazes me. When most others would have run a million miles away – you stayed, you fought and we won. I love you.

TABLE OF CONTENTS

Prologue	9
That inadequate Feeling	19
Being Angie	24
How to use this book	29
The younger years - My lessons	31
The Teenage – Tweenage years – Carving myself a backbone	42
Backpacker Angie Arrives	58
Marriage, Dogs & Business & Kids…	75
There's got to be more	117
The downward spiral	151
What's next	172

Prologue

We all go through varying degrees of shit in life. No one is perfect, it's unavoidable – get used to that fact, its not going away. But, we can choose how we react to the growing pile of sticky brown matter that surrounds us.

Our make up affects how we emotionally deal with life and dictates what actions we will take and directly affect the experiences we have.

What if we got a handle on our emotions? Would that alter our behaviours and actions and improve our ultimate experiences and outcomes?

Imagine doing a handstand and all the shit that has happened in your life falls out of your pockets onto the floor. Then you get to sift through the crap and sort out what category it fits into and consider why you held onto that particular thing for so long and if you put it back in or not (after all, it is in your pocket – right? You did hold onto it).

Memories are a mixture of good and bad, what they do is teach us how to deal with that thing the next time it crops us, it's the only way we learn. But what it does, that we all subconsciously do, is that it builds up barriers and develops warning signals so you can prepare for the next time that thing might happen. Example: You burn your hand on the kettle which means next time you are more careful, it's how we learn. You trip over a rock whist training for a big race, and chip a bone in your ankle so you now avoid running on rocky paths. You get pickpocketed in Paris, which means the next time you go there, you avoid those fucking Gypsie's and bury your wallet deep, deep into your backpack (fuckers).

See our experiences and how we react to them craft us into the humans that we are today. Therefore if you feel defensive or are cautious about a specific thing, chances are there's a reason for that.

Do yourself a favour, find a wall, do a handstand, see what shit falls out and throw away the unnecessary baggage you've been weighed down with for so long.

This book takes you on a journey through my first 40 odd years of life and re discovers some of the more memorable experiences I've had, as well as some memories I'd rather forget and works out what some of the lessons were that I learnt along the way. It's helped me to work out who I am, why I am the way I am and how to not repeat the same mistakes time and time again, because I'm starting to bore myself with the same old shit - something's got to give.

At the end of each story I pose a few questions so you can see if you can draw any comparisons with your life. I've left a bit of space for you to write down your findings too, essentially my therapy has turned into your therapy. Hey who knows you might even enjoy the process of your "unpacking".

What is your make up?

We are all human, I don't care if you are the CEO or the Cleaner, we all matter, we all have feelings and we all have lives.

Every single person on this planet wants something. What is it? Well, mostly, they want a variety of things from this list.

Success	Health
Money	Courage
Love	Security
Happiness	Freedom
Energy	Stuff
More time	Accolades
To be thanked	Travel
To be enough	Power
To Lose weight	Balance
Strength	Passion
To live longer	To be heard
Belief	Respect
Contentedness	Fame
Knowledge	Admiration

Which of these resonate with you? What do you want out of life?
Tick all that apply

First thing to note here:
These are all personal goals. This is about you, not your partner, kids or family. It's about you because quite frankly when it comes down to working out what you want out of life, you're the only person you should be listening to. Opinions are like arseholes, everyone has got one, but that doesn't mean that other people get to vomit their opinion onto you and you certainly don't have to listen.

From the above list – this is what makes me tick.

- Happiness
- Love
- Contentedness
- Health
- To Be Thanked
- To Be Enough
- Freedom
- Travel
- Passion
- Strength
- Courage

I'm not after a life filled with stuff, tons of cash, fame or accolades, that isn't what makes me purr. I quite simply just want to be happy, to love and be loved, to have the strength to get through my own variety of shit and the courage to stand up for myself during those shitty moments, to be thanked when I help people or do a great job, to be considered as more than enough and not feel like I'm fucking inadequate (because I do, most of the time - more on that shortly). I want to learn from my mistakes and be comfortable with being wrong (because I am – and often). I want to travel and be free and I want to live a life doing things I'm passionate about. I love to write, draw, make pottery, play the guitar, run, swim, do triathlons, play with my kids, hang with my hubby, that is what makes me happy.

I run my own business and yes I like it (most of the time). But work doesn't define me, work "enables" me. It was the other way around for a long time but I can now see that working my tail off for 70 hours a week to get a huge wage and not seeing daylight is not appealing and working in a corporate job sounds downright hideous (I never did go corporate). These days the idea of working for someone else sends shivers of repulsion down my spine. But that's me, you are you. You decide who you are. My meditation teacher said something great the other day and it will stay with me – "you do you and I'll do me". It's my new motto.

Talking about work defining us, its funny you know, we spend a lot our lives at work or learning at school but those are not the things that seem to spur us into song. Just turn on the radio and listen. Song after song we hear unrequited love sonnets being belted out of our speakers. The main topic is how hurt we are when love goes wrong, how unjustly we have been treated, how love is the most important thing we have, how much we want, need, regret love and the experience it gives us. How happy we all just want to be and we will apparently be happiest when that person we love realises that we love them and they love us back. (Excuse me while I vomit). Yet each time we love, we let a little less of ourselves out, all because the last time we were hurt - or so the songs are telling us anyway. But that is just life, its an experience with another lesson you've woven to fill your rich tapestry of your life story. Don't be frightened of pain, it helps to carve you - read on you'll see.

What I'm saying is that you just don't hear songs about filing paperwork, cleaning floors, writing blogs or building websites, constructing buildings or fabricating steelwork. The closest you might get is about "working hard for the money" and even that is about how she feels about it or that chick in the 80's who wailed about working 9 to 5 and how pissed off she was about working in a male dominated space. Invest yourself into things that matter. Spending inordinate amounts of time at work doing something you'll never be proud of is quite frankly, fucking stupid. Maybe find a job that is truly your passion or find something else to do that makes you purr.

When you are thinking about your list of values, add love in there, but combine it with courage and strength. We are human, we will all go through shit, your shit might be more stinky than your best mate who seems to have all her fucking ducks in a row, but her shit still stinks, let me tell you.

Set your own goals

Everyone strives for something better, the next thing, more and more and more. It's fucking exhausting but it's the game we are playing in this day and age.

So what do YOU want?
Why?
Is it that important and if so, how the hell so you intend to get it?

Here's a good thing to do to help work out what makes you tick, simply write down your qualities, strengths, weaknesses, goals, your purpose and what it is that you are looking for in this life as you? Then think about what you want to improve on?

Whatever you do needs to fuel the end user – be that yourself, your family, your colleagues or your customers and it needs to be wanted, desired or coveted.

The idea is to improve on what you already have; we are all in search of that elusive "more" or "next evolutionary step and that might actually be "less". I guess the quest for "more" is just human nature (although I bloody wish at times, that it wasn't). Whatever you decide to do as your next step, the next level, the next big thing it should be an improvement, otherwise, why would you want it? And it is ok to want to be more by accumulating less; actually, I think you might find it rather therapeutic.

STRENGTHS What are you good at?	**WEAKNESSES** What could you be better at?
GOALS What do you want to achieve out of life?	**PURPOSE** What do you think you are here to do?

In order to have all the thanks, security, wealth, success and freedom in the world you need to be good at what you do, love what you do and exude passion for whatever it is that you are doing and the rest will follow.

Question: What are you good at?

In order to be good at what you do you need to give, be that your time to your family, staff or self, you need to learn – so you'll need to continually educate, and you'll need to give yourself and the people around you time to blossom and that requires patience. You cannot expect to train and then miraculously immediately get results. Its like planning to run a marathon, most people don't just go out and run 42.2kms, they set a plan in place and chip away at improving their technique, increasing their endurance, maybe investing in some decent running shoes, shifting the extra weight, improving times, running for longer and longer without hurting themselves and then they do the marathon – see: time, education, patience and often - money.

I guess what I'm trying to say is that if you truly want something, its going to take some effort so make sure that you do actually want this magical thing and that its not just a nice idea. Make sure it's your idea, it won't feel right if it's not your idea, wait for the tingle, the gut feeling, that confirmation and only then proceed. You know what I'm talking about. It's that single moment when you know that what you are doing is 100% right, its knowing that the idea that just attached itself to you is for you and you alone.

To get "that" feeling you need to relax and let the good things flow towards you, sometimes when we try so hard, we block the good from coming to us. Have a focus, a passion and set some goals and work on them, but not to the detriment of your fun, your health or your character. Sometimes relaxing and letting things happen is the best course of action, otherwise we seem to create blocks. Most importantly – be yourself, don't compromise on who you are to impress someone else. You set YOUR goals, not their goals. You are you, not anyone else. Some people like to persuade you into doing things that might not be what you'd normally do, now there is nothing wrong with enthusiasm and encouragement in fact, I'm all for it, but there is something wrong with manipulation and coercion. Some people just want you to be like them so they feel better about themselves. I don't know about you but I'd hate to meet a clone of me, I like being unique.

You know what I say to people who try to make you into a clone of themselves? "Fuck off" is what I say, "go and pick on someone without a brain, personality or the guts to walk their own path in life, leave me alone – I'm not your puppet". Then mean it and do your own thing – you can you know.

I read a book called Big Magic a few years back, in it Elizabeth Gilbert the author describes how she believes ideas work and this page of text changed the way I look at how we work as humans and how important it is to take opportunities presented to us.

On page 2 of her "Enchantment" chapter Elizabeth describes how she thinks that ideas are another form of energy. They exist as separate entities to us lowly "humans" but they consciously choose a human vessel to attach themselves to in order to come into existence. So the idea interacts with us when we are ready. Here's the thing though, if we don't help that idea to be "made manifest" it buggers off and goes and finds another human to attach itself to. So that invention you had in your head and you did bugger all with just made millions on the latest and greatest inventors show and you sit there in your flannos and ugg boots drowning in your own misery flavoured cold milky tea.

I love this concept, I love the fact that an idea sits by our sides until we are ripe, ready to take action, or that the idea has chosen us to be the vessel to make it real in this earthly realm. So it is our job as the chosen vessel to pay attention to the signs, to be aware of the tingles, the light bulb moments, the moments when you just know that your idea is a cracker. This is the time that you know that you have been chosen, its then up to you to make it happen. How exciting!

Being a decent human isn't rocket science, but there is a science behind it. If you can understand how human emotions work and why we behave the way we do, you'll get further than most. If you can understand who you are, what you want and why you've responded to life's lessons the way you have you'll be better for it as you'll start to see patterns and you'll understand why you do what you do.

So listen, watch, pay attention because the answers are right in front of you, all you have to do is think about the lessons you have learnt from your life so far and see what you have deduced as a result. You'll see a pattern and identify core gaps that you can then work on and perhaps you might not repeat your worst mistakes – we can only hope!

That inadequate feeling...

I'm fed up of feeling inadequate... Fuck what does that even mean? The word inadequate suggests that I'm in fact equating myself to something; I don't even know what that thing is, so how can I be not it? It's a frustrating human thing we all do; we measure ourselves up against shit that isn't real or even measurable. So now I have to work out what my metric value system is and what I'm not equating to so I can ensure that my emotional suffering is actually worth the effort and time I give it to thrive.

When I was younger my inadequacies were centred around not being cool enough, I was at times a quiet kid, at times a complete loon and at times just going through the motions, so was pretty much "in neutral". I'd look at the other kids and wish I fitted in with them, with no real idea why I felt that way. I didn't have any actual evidence to suggest that perhaps they didn't want me to fit it, I just felt that way. Inadequate! And so that was the card I played. I can see now how those behaviours have stuck, and yet perhaps a variety of reasons, I'm still playing the same cards, from the same deck I had as a child.

As I turned into a teenager my inadequacies morphed into things like: I'm not pretty enough. I've never felt like a pretty girl, so instead of actually trying to improve that I dressed down, never wore makeup and really worked on that emotion. It's almost as though I took the concept of how I thought I looked and multiplied it by ten.

As an adult, I still feel most like myself when I'm wearing my blundestone boots, a pair of knackered old jean shorts and a singlet with no make up, a cap on and sunnies to hide my eyes. I have massaged my internal dialogue about the idea of "I'm not pretty" to mold myself into who I am today. It has taken 42 years for me to concede that I do look nice in a dress (sometimes with boots), and that wearing makeup (albeit only a smidgen) does actually look nice and to accept that when I bother to go and get my hair done at the hairdressers I look remarkably less like a hooker with overgrown roots and bushy eyebrows.

When I travelled as a 20 year old I was comfortable and warm inside my skin by then so the inadequate monster metamorphosed from I'm not pretty enough into 'I'm not hippie enough'. A lot of people who travelled in the late 90's tried really hard to be 'alternative'. With their dreadlocks, slightly sun kissed features, baggy cotton pants and worn out singlets that could probably fall off at the tiniest of flicks - that somehow looked great on them and made me look like I'd been dragged through a bush backwards. They had tattoos or henna adorning their bodies and carried cool satchels and they walked like they were floating. They owned their stature and other "cool" beings flocked to their sides "needing" to soak up their obviously alluring energies. Ugh!!

The concept of trying hard at something never even occurred to me. I knew I'd look like a fucking fool in that get up so in true Angie fashion, I didn't even bother. I had given up any notion of actually feeling like I belonged to anywhere or anything, and just got on with life inside my own shell. But, determined not to stay stuck inside one stationary shell forever, I decided to become a hermit crab. I'd take my unpretty formless body and relocate it (without decoration or modification) into a new location and see how my inadequacies faired in the new place for a bit. Sometimes I'd be fine for ages, sometimes the shell would scratch or hurt, sometimes it had too many parts that pinched and I'd leave that shell and locate another one that felt easier. So always in search of this elusive 'right fit', I've been wandering the planet trying to see where I might belong without ever actually trying to fit into anything.

When children came along the "I'm not a good enough mum" demon popped her head up to say G'day and as soon as she did, I hit 'Struggle Town'. A depression seeped into my mind and everything got dark for a while. Despite being reassured by so many people that I was a good mum - I'd question it.

Trying to run a full-time marketing business from home with five staff and look after two babies under 18 months was in itself a massive challenge, but I thought I should be able to handle all that, and then some. How wrong I was. If I had conceded defeat and put my hand up and said "help" things may be different today. Instead I harboured deep seeds of resentment. Particularly towards those 'yummy mummies' whose lives seemed to gush with ease, and to my husband, despite his numerous and unwavering attempts to help steer me towards doing things for myself. Even my employees who just came to work and swanned in and out without the pressure of having to keep the business afloat amidst dirty nappies and sleepless nights. I was turning myself into a wreck and it was all self created.

Failing to move past the childhood feelings of not fitting in, followed by the teenage angst of 'not pretty enough', then the traveler version of myself being not hip enough, and finally convincing myself I was not the worlds greatest mum, I had the weight of the world on my shoulders and I kept it all to myself in a glass jar. The thing about glass jars is that you can see through them. Everyone did and my emotion was clearly etched on my face - I was turning into 'Angry Angie'. I'd play the sarcastic bitch card, alongside the nonchalant "I don't really care what people think of me" card whilst wearing my "this is who I am and if you don't like it fuck off outfit" everyday.

As a result I'd repel people. Sure I'd have some friends but mostly they'd come and go. I've noticed that people "like" me but a lot of people don't really want me to be their friend so I don't get invited to much, they seem to steer away from me and I'm not surprised I've made myself into the person I am, but I had a choice.

Life is full of choices and I have carved myself into who I am. I could have tried to fit in at school, but I didn't. Instead of avoiding the shops and girlee trips my friend Sarah used to try to drag me on, I could have embraced them and tried the clothes on, let her do my hair and makeup and taught myself to feel "prettier" but I didn't. When I travelled, I could have morphed myself into whomever I felt like, to try and "find myself" by getting outside of my skin, but I didn't. Instead I just wandered aimlessly around the world looking at life through my normal coloured glasses and seeing what there was to see. When kids came I could have joined the mothers' group and shared my parental stresses with other women, I could have made like-minded friends. Instead I saw them as annoying and quite frankly I'd rather stick pins in my eyes than go to a 'mothers group' (ugh!). I went to one group once knowing that I'd hate it, hey and guess what I did - I hated it, because I told myself to hate it. Fucking idiot - honestly.

Now as a mum of two beautiful boys who have thankfully not been too scarred by my inability to try new things and be a little bubblier, I can see that I'm still making some dumb mistakes. I want to acknowledge these and move past them instead of bottling them up and building a case against myself and making myself feel like I'd be better off if I didn't exist.

See no one cares if I don't fit in, apart from me, no one cares that I don't feel pretty, apart from me, no one gives a shit if I am hip, only me and no one cares if I am a marginally better Mum because most people see me as a good Mum already. So, when the feeling of I'm not good enough came up again recently after a conversation with my husband I knocked it on the head. It's time to stop this shit and pull my head out of my arse.

During my late thirties and early 40's I've struggled with a bit of depression and have taken an antidepressant pill, which recently I stopped taking because I wanted my feelings to be real not blurred out in any way shape or form. I've made some errors in judgment and have landed myself on hot water and they were all based on the "I'm not enough/adequate" principle.

Well it's time to stop this shit: I AM ENOUGH!. I am adequate. If I'm going to measure myself against anything it'll be my mistakes, because those are the things that have helped me to grow. Those mistakes are what I don't want.

When I'm not being my best I can only get better so instead of beating myself up, I'll use those experiences as my measuring stick of what not to do.

I'm not inadequate, I'm equitable to myself and only myself because I don't want to be you or anyone else. – Like Oscar Wilde once said – Be yourself, everyone else is taken. Finally, I want to be simply 'me'.

This means working at being the best version of me I can be. I'll use my own life experience to judge my behaviours and myself.

Along my journey of self-discovery, I have learned a few big things, and I'm going to share those with you. I am writing this book, because one of the biggest things I have finally learned, and understand, is that everything I've just detailed over the past few pages, all those feelings and experiences, are not unique to me. I've started having conversations with other people who all feel or have felt exactly the same way at times. They are part of the 'me too' brigade that can empathise with exactly how I felt, at various ages and stages of their lives.

So I know I'm not writing this, and you're not reading this, because I'm having unique experiences. We all go through long, and sometimes multiple, periods of our lives where we feel inadequate.

So let's talk about this shit. We all need to get better at acknowledging our fears, facing up to our inadequacies and looking at them head on and seeing if they really are realistic.

In reality, only you care enough about you to look that deep anyway, everyone else is running around this floating rock we call home trying to work out who they are and sifting through their own crap.
You're enough, get on with being enough and improve on your enoughness as life's challenges hit you square in the face, just don't forget your lessons along the way or you'll just re play them till you do.

Being Angie

From a young age I've lived in my own world, it's not a bad place, in fact it's a great place. I occasionally have to leave my "little world" and play the game we call life with all the other humans, but essentially I like my little realm and I'm happy hanging out there.

Always content with my own company, as a child my parents and siblings thought I was kind of weird, but I was perfectly happy. Growing up in South East London, we lived in a big community block of red brick flats on Pomeroy Street, New Cross. I remember sitting on the window ledge of the bedroom I shared with my two sisters for hours at a time, just watching the world go by. It never occurred to me to not do that or that people might think that there was something wrong - I was just being me. This was my space, my place where my imagination could run away with me.

I'm not dissimilar today; I still like (and mostly prefer) my own company. Don't get me wrong I'm not agoraphobic I like going outside, in fact I'm happier in a forest somewhere, nor do I have Anthropophobia I like socialising and meeting new people, I guess I'm just comfortable with my own company and do not feel the need to incessantly talk and be heard...

I was never very "cool" but then I never really tried to be anything else. Maybe it all started at secondary school where I always felt "judged". Some of the other kids "picked" on me, not physically (often) but verbally, calling me names and stealing my bag to throw it around the school playground, stupid stuff like that. I guess they didn't like the fact that because I listened to the teacher in class, that I was smarter than them, so I earned the nickname "Boffin". It was really annoying and at the time I disliked it immensely, but I did learn to deal with it. Maybe that where I perfected my "fuck off look". I attended an all girls' school in South East London, it was a normal state/public school, and the uniform was brown with a brown and yellow striped tie and a cream shirt – yuck! (the school uniform designer needed a bullet in his/her head for that). Looking back and thinking about some of these girls who picked on me and their homelives makes me understand why they felt the need to control my life because their home life was so out of control for them, so this was how they got their power back.

At the time I dealt with the situation by walking away and retreating. I rarely stuck up for myself but occasionally I did and when I did they all looked at me as though I had lost the plot (possibly, because I had). Today I'm less of a push over but I can definitely see that some of these behaviours have stuck. I still retreat and bottle up my annoyance to "literally burst" when I'm finally ready to speak/ shout up. Although of late I'm trying to work on removing this rather debilitating quality as it really doesn't help.

I've never been the type of person to have a single friend or group of friends to confide in/moan to. I do have mates, but my friends are fluid, they come and go. I do not get attached to any one person often. I'm ok with that. I've got a few mates that I've known for many years and when we see each other its just like old times, but really I can make connections easily and be just as happy to see them or not.

For a long time I found it hard to be friendly with women, some of them annoyed me with their fakeness and incessant need to moan about fucking rubbish, so I befriended men. That was great, but sometimes the men got the relationship all mixed up in their heads – but really, that was their issue and most of the time I'd happily tell them so and life would move on. Admittedly there have been glitches in that theory though.

As I have gotten older and kids have come along, these days I have more female friends who are parents of the kids they have been to school with, we all seem to have the same outlook and similar hurdles. I still feel like a misfit though, even with them. I have a handful of good female friends who I can really talk to and that's really about it. I'm ok with that, anymore than that and I'd drive myself bonkers anyway.

My Mum always said to me that she wanted to raise three "independent young women" well she did that. I'm so independent that I don't feel like I need anyone's help. It's a mistake, I do, and I need to accept help graciously. I'm still learning that lesson.

As a mum, wife and businesswoman I have a hectic life. Constantly on the go, we hardly ever "stop" and so the need to work as a team is imperative, but my strong willed "I can do it all" behaviour actually holds us back. It drives my husband crazy, it also drives me crazy but how do you undo everything you've ever learnt?

It's a lesson that I want to unpack and work out. It's what stops me and it's likely what is stopping you as well.

I own a Marketing Consultancy, I have 5 staff who work a majority of the time for me, but they also work for other companies too, we all work satellite, so we all work from the comfort of our own homes. I designed it that way so I didn't have to be in an office and be in charge of people. So I'm in charge of clients and their projects and the people make the projects happen, its better that way. I feel much less like a counselor this way and it's much more cost effective and I am free (one of my core values).

We did all work in an office for a few years but it drove me insane. Apart from the team "talking" constantly, it actually made us less productive. I find the need to constantly talk rather annoying, I like to work in silence, so the constant "buzz and hum" of chitter chatter chiseled away at my sanity. So when the time came to move house, I decided that we would all work from our own homes and its much, much better. Having two young children I also fit in being "mummy" around my business.

My master plan was to start a business I could work from home whilst I raised two children - so far so good. I never was a particularly good employee; I could always see a better way that the employers couldn't (it's a very self indulgent opinion I have of myself - I know). In my opinion, my employers as far as I could see, were all very good at meeting and telling other people what to do but not giving them any tools/budget to carry out the job, then complaining when they don't meet their targets. So my team are free to suggest changes, make changes and I give them what they need to do their jobs. They are free to come and go and they are paid for what they do, so it is all very transparent and it's a much better culture.

I also wanted to ensure that I had continuous work whilst I had young kids and not be held by the short and curlies by someone else's sodding company rules. I didn't want to be told when I could have maternity leave and when I could come back to work or not. I'm not very good at being told what to do and so working for myself was a much better solution.

Now I'll never be able to go back and work as an employee again as I've seen the light! Mind you it's not been easy and I'm not earning millions, but I've never lost money and I've never not been able to provide. Good job that I'm not after that big pay packet, I'd rather be happy and free than loaded and knackered. Just remember, having your own business is not the lucrative cash cow you might imagine, its fucking hard work and you have to be prepared to put time into the project as a constant.

However, back to the unpacking.
My nature is to "get on with it and do it" I'm from the generation where you needed to get on with it if you wanted something to work. I saw my Dad strive to get on with it with his plumbing business and my Mum who is my total inspiration she raised 3 girls, worked in two part time jobs and studied at Uni to become a teacher whilst staying sane. After qualifying, she quickly took on leadership roles and stepped into the Headmistress Role where she excelled at turning poorly performing schools into thriv-

ing over achieving schools. So I am from a family of battlers, leaders and entrepreneurs it is just what we've always done so being my own boss and leading is not alien to me, its just what we do.

I started working part time at age 11 in the community garden in the block of flats where I grew up in New Cross, London. I loved this job; it played up to my escapism in nature requirement. When I hit 13 & ¾ (some idiot set this age) I was legally allowed to get a "real part time job" and so for a few years I worked on a Market stall in Peckham Rye selling men's clothing. I earned a fair amount of money for a teenager who didn't actually spend much and so I contributed towards the shopping at times, I was happy to do this as well, it made me feel like I had purpose and that I could help.

So to suddenly start accepting help seems a little alien to me. I'm the backbone; I'm the one that holds this shit together, apart from when I fall apart. Then the shit literally hits the fan and I am left looking bewildered and sheepish when I make daft and sometimes monumental mistakes. Then I try to do too much in an unrealistic timeframe and fail epically. So, learn Angie, its OK to ask for help, to point out a problem and to get help and be grateful for it.... And breathe...

How to use this book

This book is like therapy for me, but I meet so many people that have had similar experiences to me, but they haven't dissected the lessons that the experience gave. My school of thought is that we are born into this body (for me – as Angie), we are here to learn a set of lessons and then move on to your next existence. If you don't learn the lesson you just keep repeating the same old shit until you accept the lesson and move up the great big ladder of life. So I guess its about being conscious of who you are, what you do, why you do the things you do and what you should be learning from these experiences.

So the next section of this book will detail some of the biggest decisions that I have made and essentially what my memory allows me to recall (its not that great these days) and what I believe the lesson was in it all.

I have left some room at the end of each section for you to write your own memories, and dissect them to identify the lessons you should learn from that experience. It will help you to assimilate everything you have been through that has been of consequence (good or bad) and allow you to really reflect on why you are the way you are and why you do what you do. It'll be therapeutic, believe me...

Decisions that make a monumental difference
Think back...

In your life there will have been times that you made definitive decisions that have shaped the course of your life to date. Miraculously even though my memory is somewhat faulty, I remember most of my monumental decisions times and what each of them meant to my life today. I call these my IME moments. IME means "In My Experience" because this whole book is based on my experiences and my lessons, but you may draw comparisons with them.

These are my conscious decisions that have sculpted my life and essentially shaped who I am. As you read these, take a moment to think about the conscious decisions you have made and why you made them. Then reflect upon the lessons you might have learnt from your decisions. You hold the key to unlocking the secret to your own strategy to take the next step in your evolutionary journey. Pay attention because you already know all the answers.

The younger years - My lessons

IME MOMENT:
Self Sabotage - Age 8 (I started early)

My sister Nikki would walk my younger sister Jojo and I home when Mum was working. These were the days when we felt free, we'd stop at the sweet shop at "the common" on the way home and spend our 20p that we have saved all day long and burned a hole in our pockets, waiting for that moment when we could get a wham bar and a mix up and slowly amble our way back home through the park, past the housing estate where the "cool kids" hung out. My big sister was 18months older than me and she was always more social than me. She'd "hang out" with some of these kids sometimes.

I was a pain in the bum to my big sister because just as the cool kids came into view I'd run up to them, just close enough for them to be able to see us all, jump up in the air and lie on the floor and stay as still as I could for enough time to make them look at me, to Nikki and then laugh. I'm not sure why I purposefully wanted to look stupid maybe to embarrass my sister. I think she wanted to be considered cool and I had no time for it (In my head - I was never going to be "cool" anyway).

Today I still purposefully sabotage perfectly normal situations to make myself feel like I just don't belong and it's ok not to do something. It's dumb, its like I'm making excuses for myself to not do something that could be really good for me. But no in my head my dialogue says – "I'll never be cool, so why try, so lets damage any chance of anyone ever liking me". So dumb...I'm 42 and I've just stopped doing this. Don't let self-sabotage ruin any chance you have of shining the way you could and should.

LESSON I HAVE LEARNT:
Give people a chance. Try new things. Don't piss people off just to try and get out of doing something out of the ordinary. If I can pass on any wisdom, it's that if you try and have a go, you'll be so surprised at what you can achieve when you put your mind to it.

Ask Yourself:

When was the last time you self sabotaged a situation because you thought you'd be incapable or wouldn't fit in?

When you look back at your childhood, do you see any patterns from this childhood memory in your life today?

Do you still hold onto your childhood behaviours? If so what are they?

IME MOMENT:
To start my own car washing then window washing business at the age of 10

As I've mentioned, as a child I grew up on a community block of flats in New Cross, South East London. It was a time when there was trouble on the streets, but nothing that wasn't out of the ordinary. You'd hear of bad stuff happening, but take it in your stride. From an early age I learned to be street-wise and be aware of what not to do and where not to go. Because we were savvy we were gifted the chance to stand on our own two feet pretty early on in life.

We were also taught the value of money at a young age and so at age 10 my little sister and I decided to start up our own car washing enterprise. This was my first foray into business and marketing. We had to make our own flyers, print them (at our school where Mum also worked at) and deliver them to all 75 flats in the block where we lived, then take orders and finally deliver the service.

We had it all under control, we'd have the radio blaring songs of the era like 'Come on Eileen' by Dexy's Midnight Runners, the buckets were full of soapy water, the sponges were clean and ready and we had a queue of customers. Every Saturday and Sunday we'd get out there for a few hours and while away the day earning a few pounds. It was great, we felt like we were such amazing entrepreneurs and to be fair at such a young age, we were.

The Car Washing was going well but then the local boys on the block decided to come in and undercut us in price! (Bastards) But instead of giving up, throwing a tantrum and throwing in the sponge, we opted to carve a niche in our enterprise and started washing windows instead. There were more windows to wash than cars and the boys' attention to detail was rubbish so we made loads more cash than them, plus they gave up anyway (losers). This I guess sparked my interest in being an entrepreneur, and being resilient with it. Little did I know it'd help me drive a niche into my own real enterprise some 30 years later?

LESSON I LEARNT:
Have a crack, just get on and have a go and when you reach hurdles you jump over them, diversify and find a solution.

Ask Yourself:

Have you ever come across a problem that meant that what you were doing was destroyed?

....
....
....

How did you deal with that kind of problem?

....
....
....

Did it actually destroy anything or did you manage to find a way around it?

....
....
....

Sometimes re framing the problem helps you see the silver lining – there is one, even if you cannot imagine what it might be right now. Why? Because everything happens for a reason.

Holding onto your experience and letting it make an impact on your life today is unhealthy. Perhaps consider that it is time to let it go.

IME MOMENT:
Decided not to attend church at age 11

When something feels wrong you know, I've always known that if my gut says don't do it – I should listen.

I now know (as an adult with young children) that Sundays was my Mum and Dad's chance to be "alone". At the time this was not obvious to me, so every Sunday we would be carted off to Church in a stupid dress with Nan and Granddad (log onto the website to see images of me in a frock, I hated wearing anything remotely girly). We'd hop into Granddad's Burgundy coloured Old Triumph Car and slowly trundle our way through the backstreets of Peckham sucking on aniseed balls (which I still love to this day) to keep us quiet all the way to St Francis (The Friary), the church next door to my Primary School with the same name. It was a time when Belinda Carlisle was singing about 'Heaven being a place on earth' and so I wondered why we needed to go in search of it in this place!!

The problem was that the Church service was just so boring and every week the same drivel would be inflicted upon us (or so it seemed to a child). The priest always seemed to have had a few too many sips of the wine, which made him sound like he was slurring. He'd be waffling on about some hideously thick book and reciting (badly) verses from it and then trying to talk about it like it actually mattered. As you can imagine my ability to focus on this blathering fool in a dress and patterned scarf at the front was limited. The religion or the message was not what offended me;

it was just so boring, long and incomprehensible. So one day I distinctly remember, bold as brass walking into the living room at home after a particularly boring church trip and saying to my Mum. "Mum I don't want to go to Church anymore". Miraculously, her response was "That's fine Honey but you have to go over and tell your Nan and Granddad that yourself".

So at age 11, over I march (they only lived over the road) and I told them. In the small kitchen of their town house they stood listening to me. I think they were slightly taken aback but they took it well and my sisters had this huge look of relief on their faces, as they stood behind me waiting for the fall out that never came. They hated church too but had never said anything.

LESSON I LEARNT:
That it is ok to have my own opinion and that voicing it did not mean I was going to be punished, it just meant that I needed to face it myself. Kudos goes to my Grandparents for their calmness and also to my parents for allowing me to make the decision without fearing their reprisal. But then they avoided the Church like the plague so it would not have been a very convincing argument anyway.

I did end up taking myself back to Sunday school to go through confirmation to see if I could re connect, which to a point I did. But I seriously wondered why religion had to be delivered in such a boring "listen to me or I shall strike you down" kind of way.

More recently I've reconnected spiritually rather than through a "God" as such. I now believe there is a physical existence and there is a spiritual realm and the veil between the physical and the spiritual is thinner than we think which means communication can happen through time and space and we can learn from this exponentially.
Its strange to think that as a child I was taught that God was a HE and that HE sets the rules, but as an adult I've discovered that God is not a

being, it (not HE) is a concept, an energy, a universal force that resides in all of us and we can choose to pay attention to it or not. God is not is an old guy with a beard sitting on a cloud looking down on us and judging our behaviour as his little minions. Church needs updating in my opinion and re framing for our fast-paced world that doesn't understand old-fashioned parables.

Here's an idea why doesn't someone start a church based on the values of "you are not the single most important thing on this fucking planet" aimed at young people so they grow into responsible adults instead of idiots. Then our next generation might stand a chance.

With the Ten Commandments being

- Self respect and the respect of others and their property is the most important rule
- Selfies are unimportant and pouting makes you look stupid
- Life is not going to be handed to you on a silver platter at the age of 25+ its time to move out of home and make your ow way in the world. Laziness is a disease.
- Your voice does not need to be loud to be heard
- Driving like a twat doesn't make you cool – put the phone down
- Working your way up from the bottom is just how life goes
- Expecting to get stuff all the time is not how life works, stuf costs money – go earn it
- The art of getting out of bed and trying hard is how to succeed
- The accumulation of stuff will not make you happy
- Be fucking grateful

Ask Yourself:

When was the last time that you felt that something was wrong in your gut but you knew that admitting it might hurt someone's feelings?

Have you ever had trouble verbalising your own opinion, which has resulted in you making yourself do something you didn't actually want to do? How did that make you feel? Its probably better not to repeat that.

You know we all wish we could take back our power at some stage in our lives and we all just want to say what we think, sometimes we can't because its mean and uncalled for but sometimes we can.

IME MOMENT:
To work for the local gardener, where I felt like I was in my own world. Age 11

My first job was fabulous. I worked for Bob – the local gardener/caretaker for our community block of flats as his sidekick. He was a 30 - 40 year old man who had some vague understanding of hygiene but not quite enough to secure him any kind of girlfriend. He was a nice guy, I got along with him and thankfully he wasn't a weirdo, just a guy working in a garden that needed someone to help and I was his helper. I loved this job, it was dirty and all about hard labour. I liked feeling like I'd done a good days work. I would plant and dig and mow and weed and paint and clean and it was great. I remember one summer holiday painting all of the shed doors on the block with thick black gloss paint, I can still smell it.

Today I still like getting stuck into gardening and when my hubby is short handed on site, I muck in and chuck my Blundstones, a singlet and a pair of shorts on and get cracking, it's the best feeling. Women who think that hard work is beyond them are beyond me. I don't get it. Worrying about your sodding nails and hair when you can get so much satisfaction from shovelling a pile of mulch. I guess that's just the way I am.

We recently bought our first bit of acreage and I get the most fun out of chopping trees and making bonfire piles, collecting fruit and nuts from the trees, growing veggies, feeding the ducks and chooks and generally pottering about.

Anyway, I digress, we had a gardening shed which was one of the rooms near the community flat that was on the other side of the block of flats. It was the size of a small living room, but had enough space for tools, plants and fertiliser. I had my own bench space there and I loved it. I loved the smell of the mud, the wet plants and the rawness and dirtiness of the room. I would put up loads of posters (mostly of The Pink Panther rather than boy bands) and listen to the music I loved, I distinctly remember dancing to 'The Walk of Life' in there one day and getting sprung, Dire Straits were one of my favourite bands as a child, which is a little left of field when all of my friends were into Bros and wearing Grolsch bottle top on their ugly black shoes. I never did like being into the "popular things". Some things never change.

One day Bob handed me a gift as a thank you for my hard work, he had hand drawn an image from "The Little Prince", an amazing story that I still love to this day. Looking back I think I would have liked Bob as an adult, not in any way romantically but as a human. We always had good conversations; he was an artist, a gentle soul and a gardener. It's nice to have memories of decent humans you meet along your life's journey and he is one of the good ones.

LESSON I LEARNT:
Don't judge a book by its cover. Bob wasn't rich or the most hygienic person but he had a good soul and he fed my need to be alone and work. Being a loner, this job was perfect for me; we could both just be in our own little gardening worlds. Being alone in nature is where I find my solace, it's the only place that calms me and makes me feel connected.

Ask Yourself:

When was the last time that you looked at someone and judged them on their appearance?

Can you remember a time when you felt that you were judged unfairly?

Name the one place where you found your solace as a child

Have you ever found that one place that makes you feel at peace? If not, this is your quest, you need to find it. In that space you will find your soul waiting with open arms applauding your resilience, in this place you will be able to locate your true hidden self. Then you will be calm.

Review your younger childhood years
So as this section comes to an end I ask you to go back to your findings about your qualities, strengths, weaknesses, goals and purpose and see if any of the experiences you have had during your younger childhood years are affecting your life right now?

What childhood experiences immediately spring to mind as life changing moments for you? Should your experiences still be affecting you today?

....

....

....

Are you happy for them to be still affecting the way you behave?

....

....

....

Can you see any patterns that you started to develop as a child?

....

....

The teenage – tweenage years carving myself a backbone

IME MOMENT:
Childhood Judgment and the effects it had on me...

I guess I've always wanted to achieve. Never happy to just be ordinary, I've always felt that there has to be more. I loved learning and reading and found that if I was learning, essentially I could ignore the outside world (to a point).

Part of my make up is to gain the approval from other people. The term "people pleaser" makes me shudder, but I guess that's what I am. It's a trait I dislike in myself and has essentially held me back from being freer. Why? Because I've always felt like I'm not enough, instead of just being who I am and accepting what is. Part of me always strives for the next achievement and to be quietly noticed by the people that matter for it, which in a way is why I am where I am and why I've managed to achieve what I have, however it is also quite debilitating, always seeking the approval of someone else, someone who I thought had an opinion that mattered. I constantly feel that it might be better to go and live in the woods where no other humans exist and just write, and maybe that's why I now live on property with my own trees and I write... hmmm

Back at school, I would worry about what the teacher thought of me, so when I was sure I knew the answer in class, I'd pop my hand up straight away, when I was almost but not 100% sure I never would even think about putting my hand up because I hated being told I was incorrect instead of just having a go. Interestingly I see this trait in my eldest son Jake now, so I'm trying to get him to have a go anyway and not fall into the trap of always needing to be right.

As another school based example, let me tell you a story. Picture me aged 5 sitting in the infant class, school was all very new at that stage and I wanted my teachers to like me. One day we had a substitute teacher come to the classroom – Mrs. White, she was a hard-nosed bitch (from the tender memory of a 5 year old). Her small but solid stature, jet black hair with her fixed angry stare made me fear her. That day I was sitting in my small plastic moulded grey chair with my back straight and listening ears on (at age 5 you already hate me - right!). The girl sitting next to me "Shareen" starts to talk just as Mrs. White starts to explain what we are doing. I lean over to Shareen and ask her to be quiet because I cannot hear. Next thing I know the witch at the front of the class is calling my name out at the top of her lungs from the blackboard and she only fucking sends me to the headmaster's office to sit on the black square. I felt so singled out and unfairly treated. It's a memory that I've had in my pocket for 37 years (I really think its time to let it go) but it does make me realise that it was quite possibly the catalyst for my "need" to never be singled out again, to never be publicly humiliated.

It explains my absolute hatred of confrontation and my dislike for telling other people off. As a mother I have had to get over this as children need verbal instructions and sometimes need to be told to stop being little pricks (sometimes in my angry witch voice too)...

Scarily my eldest son told me a story recently about his fill in teacher putting him in the corner and then again on the same day he got placed on the mat for speaking in class even though he feels it was about the task they were doing. I believe him. Jake never gets in trouble; he is just a really conscientious child. I just hope that he doesn't harbour the anger from the public humiliation for as long as I have. How do you go about re teaching your kids how to deal with confrontation when you are really shit at dealing with it yourself? It's not easy.

It's essentially taken me 40 years and one book (this one) to unpack the fear of judgment that I have harboured for my existence as Angie so far. All my fears that I possess, I have collected from my various experiences throughout life to date. I'm not sure if I'll ever let it go completely, I'd like to think that the reigns of terror have loosened though.

LESSON:
Be good at things because YOU want to be good at them, not because you are trying to meet the expectation of someone else. Do what YOU need to do not what everyone else wants you to do, but have a go at everything otherwise you'll never know what you are great at. Don't fear the reprisal of someone else because they are not always right. Mrs. "Witchy" White was wrong and I know it – Cow!

Ask Yourself:

Has someone ever told you off for something you didn't do? Are you scarred from the experience?

....

....

....

Is there anything you want to do that you would love to try but are not sure if you'd be any good at it?

....

....

....

What holds you back in life? (Not who)

....

....

....

....

....

IME MOMENT:
Decided to avoid the playground at break time and became good at woodwork and metalwork, which channeled my creativity.

When I look back on my Secondary school days and compare with other people's stories, my experience really wasn't that bad, but just like anyone the experience in the moment is what develops the memories and what changes your actions and reactions. At the time I felt vindicated and singled out by some of the girls at school. As a loner I would wander about on my own, sure I had some friends Sarah, Erica, Mirelle and Sandra, but mostly I'd just mooch around on my own with my ear phones in (being sneaky as we weren't allowed them at school) pumping out music by Guns n' Roses and Dire Straits. Maybe that was 'weird' to the "popular" girls because they felt the need to be in a group of adoring fans constantly. Anyway the popular girls weren't that nice to me at times and so to avoid feeling like I was disliked I would hide in the woodwork room and carry on with my creative projects.

My teacher Mr. Cane let me frequent the room and he'd leave me the key to lock up afterwards. One year I made a whole series of key rings from Perspex and Wood for my family with their initials, other times I'd continue making a chair, a chessboard, or just something to fill in the time between lessons. Being alone and being creative is still a huge passion for me. I loved the smell of the Craft Design Technology room, the freshly cut wood and the smell of slightly going off PVA glue. Its funny how some memories have smells.

If I had my time at that school with those girls who occasionally ridiculed me again I'd aim to be more confident, stronger and answer them back. I wouldn't let them steal my bag or my homework and I'd probably push them back. It's funny looking at how confident I am these days and looking back at who I was years ago. It has shaped who I am, but it might have been better to not have to have felt that way during the years that could have been a more positive experience.

What makes me laugh is that years later I discovered that a couple of those girls got pregnant young, didn't finish their schooling and were leading boring existences in the same place where we grew up, whilst I had been to Uni, travelled the world and immigrated to Australia. Guess being a smart-arsed bully doesn't pay off after all.

Today, I still like to be alone and be creative, it's peaceful. I find time to draw, write and read, I play with my pottery wheel and I play my guitar and drink beer on my deck when I can. Its part of who I am and without it I'd be less.

LESSON:
Finding a way to express your creativity is great, but not to the detriment of your character. Never let anyone take your Power and squash your sense of self. Stand up, stand strong and never, never take anyone's shit. You are better than that.

Interesting fact:
I did a past life regression workshop at the age of 38, where the girls who

picked on me at school were in the crowd of villagers who were burning me at the stake for being a "witch". Guess I've always been different; guess I've always been ridiculed for it. I guess its time to let that stuff go...

Ask Yourself:

Can you remember the last time that you were made to feel less than you are?

Do you think that you were bullied when you were younger?

Have you ever taken away someone else's power to make you feel good?

Have you forgiven the perpetrators or have you been forgiven?

Do you see a pattern based on your past experiences and if you are letting those experiences shape your behaviour now?

IME MOMENT:
Decided that I would not hang around with girls when I changed schools (they were my nemesis) age 15

When I turned 15, I had to change high school; this was because the school I attended was being transformed into the Sixth Form College that I would later attend. I moved to a different school, a mixed school, and so I was introduced to boys in a school setting.

Now don't get me wrong, I was hardly sheltered and I had many boy mates, I'd even had a boyfriend or two. But this was different. Past experiences at the girl's school meant that I consciously steered myself as far away from the "popular" group of girls as possible (they were all the same, lipstick wearing, hair models who wore tight clothes and perfume to learn about Math and English. So in true Angie style I hung out with the people who were normal and weren't trying so hard to be someone else – the boys.

I did have two girl mates at this school, they were cool, but the rest of them thought far too much of themselves and essentially bored me to tears with their fakeness.

What happened was that the guys were nice to me, but not because they wanted to date me, just because they accepted me for whom I was. They were happy for me to play soccer in the playground with them, they liked the fact that I liked making stuff and liked rock music. Sure I did go to the movies / watch a band with 2 of these guys, but it was short lived and not much changed when that all ended, because they were more mates than anything else.

Hindsight thought:
Maybe that's how the boys saw me, not as "girlfriend" material just one of the lads and when they crossed the bridge to the "dark side" they ran

back to what they knew quick sharp. So I wasn't a girl's friend and I wasn't a girlfriend. I was alone in my loner world and it was all my own doing.

What this did to me in later life though was that I essentially alienated myself from the female of the species. I purposely put making friends with girls in the too hard basket and avoided them like the plague. It's something that I'm now trying to reverse. I had male friends who saw me as one of the lads and some again crossed that bridge but it would be me that scarpered to the safety of the other side this time. I had made my comfortable place and it felt strange to change it. So on I trudged through life pretty much humming to the tune of my own music. Not much has changed.

LESSON:
Hang out with people who make you feel like it's OK to be you, but don't alienate yourself.
Empower yourself with your own decisions but see that we are here to evolve at the same time.

Ask Yourself:

Do you have criteria for the people who choose to hang out with?

....

....

Do you hang only out with people who fit your criteria?

....

....

Do you think that you making decisions about who you are now that will affect who you are in the future?

IME MOMENT:
Decided that I will not be bullied, or take anyone's shit and that I will be confident when starting college age 16.

It's 1992 and I distinctly remember the walk up Belmont Hill in the back streets of Lewisham in London, (back to the old site of my 1st secondary school) on the first day of Sixth Form College with U2 blaring "One" on my Walkman. It was a fine September morning and the sun was trying its UK best to shine on my face. I remember this distinctively because it was a critical turning point in my own evolution and I could feel it (maybe it was an idea that had clung to me, a force something bigger than myself urging me to be confident and strong because this was a poignant moment that would help shape my life as I know it today). So to answer Bono – "is it getting better, or do you feel the same"? well I made fucking sure it got better and wasn't the same.

I was absolutely bloody adamant that I would not be a doormat anymore, no longer would I put up with people pushing me around, I had had enough. I had managed to be less of a push over at the last school but I was going back to the place where I had felt mediocre and inadequate and so I was wary.

I point blank refused to feel inferior and so I didn't, I pulled up my big girl britches and put on that positive mental attitude, smiled and went into College with an attitude of "this is going to be great" and do you know, it was. That mindset change has carved me into the woman that I am today. It's incredible what you can do when you set your mind to it...

Now I was the one being invited out to the local nightclub. My mate Rachel and I spent a lot of weekends at The Venue in New Cross dancing the night away swigging cider from Pint glasses and generally snogging local boys. The soundtrack to this era was Van Morrison's Brown Eyed Girl and when my sisters came along it was punctuated with Sister Sledge's "We Are Family" and Gloria Gaynor's – I Will Survive, and survive we did. Good God it was fun!

There were a bunch of "cool" kids that I knew, but some not so well. I sat on the outside of their circle, over the first few months of college, but I made an effort to get to know them and by the end of the second year of sixth form, we all went on holiday to St Tropez (France). It felt like such an achievement to go on this holiday, like I somehow fitted in, even when a lot of the time on that holiday I still felt awkward and like I was a misfit. Life is still like that.

On this holiday as a group we all decided to go out into St Tropez to the nightclubs on an organised tour as none of us were driving and we needed to get there somehow. So we went to the tour guide and booked in. It was one of those tours where you pay up front and get let in first and get given drink vouchers. Except the clubs were empty, the DJ hadn't started, the vouchers were not honoured and it was in a word "shite". We all went back to the caravan site disappointed and bored. Interestingly enough I was the only person in our group of seemingly "cool kids" who had the guts to go back to the tour guide and demand our money back. After harassing the crap out of him for a day or two he gave in and refunded us. It kind of made me realise that these teenagers that I looked up to and wanted to be like, were just scared kids themselves, it made me a much stronger person and it made them realise that I wasn't that girl who could be walked over.

We went to a bar on the night that we got our refund where a band was playing, we had seen them a few nights before playing the same set. They all bought me drinks with their refunds as we danced to The Boomtown Rats "I don't like Mondays". And the growth cycle continued.

It's funny I describe this, yet there are still groups of people that I know and I feel like I'm privileged to be in their company, like I somehow shouldn't be there and that I'm faking it. I wonder if this feeling will ever subside? Maybe that is up to me. It's me who is viewing their perception to be anything but positive. No one as ever said anything derogatory to me; in fact, it's quite the opposite, yet I still feel less. I need to get over it.

In more recent times, (2015) I attended a Heart Awakening Retreat in the Byron Bay Hills, and even there I felt like I was "mainstream" and the other people were far "cooler", "hippier", more worthy of being there than me. It took me back to my traveling days and the way I felt about fitting in then too. They were vegan, flowy pant wearing, slightly musky smelling humans with tattoos and piercings, with an insulated view of the world and a thirst for esoteric knowledge. In comparison there was me in my normal black leggings, t-shirt, hair tied back looking decidedly not alternative. A meat eating human with no tattoos (at that point) or any strange piercings I felt pretty mainstream. I left having eradicated that feeling, but its still there initially, this "I'm not enough" the "I don't fit in" feeling. Well its time to get rid of these ridiculous emotions, I am SO enough, I am me, that's who I am and not anyone else, and if people don't like that, quite frankly they can shove it sideways.

Lately I've realised that I am one strong woman and that has earned the respect of many people in my circles. Apparently people find me interesting, which both surprises me and makes me swell with pride at the same time.
Having the ability to hold a decent conversation is a huge part of it. Look I'm never going to be everyone's cup of tea, but that is perfectly ok in my book. I certainly don't like everyone I meet, (in fact I don't like many other

humans) but being able to connect with others without the small talk is great. Please note that the weather is NOT an interesting topic of conversation.

LESSON:
Your mindset is your strongest weapon, change your thoughts and you can change your world.

Watch out for people you connect really easily with – they are more connected to you than you know.

Ask Yourself:

Is there anything that makes you feel like you don't fit in with your peers?

....
....

Do you think your peers feel like they fit in with you?

....
....

When was the last time that you truly felt like you were faking it?

....
....

What is it that makes you feel like you are not enough?

....
....
....

IME MOMENT:
Decided to go to university to study architecture and then landscape architecture and then decide that I was not my life's path and withdraw age 19

I had major pre conceived ideas of what University would be like and how great it would be... Reality and my imagination did not gel particularly well. I entered Uni doing Landscape Architecture; I initially applied for "Architecture" but I really wasn't very good at Mathematics and so the Dean suggested that as I liked gardening, drawing, design and the outside that I might consider Landscape Architecture instead. I took the place and started Uni.

The University I chose was close to home and so I stayed put at home, in hindsight, I should have moved onto campus, it would have made me tether myself to the place and the course with a stronger rope.

As the months wore on, so too did the course. I started to get average results. I was used to being the top of the class and suddenly the female tutor didn't like what I was submitting. I was one of two female students in the class, the other one spoke mostly Portuguese and hung out with her Portuguese mates from other degrees in her spare time and so yet again I happily hung out with the guys in my class. Nothing weird there.

But I wasn't achieving good results and the judgment was negative I started to stumble and disassociate with the course, that, combined with the requirement to learn 50 Latin names of plants every week when my memory is like a sieve, it all became a little too hard and so I pulled out of University and went to get a job in London.

Reflection:
Looking back, I know I shot myself in the foot because Landscape Architecture is exactly what I should be doing; I would be excellent at it.

I let another person's opinion get into my head and changed the course of my life as a result. This female tutor for some reason was threatened by me, when really all I wanted to do was please her. (Vomit and eye roll)

LESSON LEARNT:
Things are laid before you for a reason, sometimes sticking to your guns is the strongest thing you can do. I guess this was one of those ideas I failed. To the idea that decided to take me to University – I'm sorry.

Ask Yourself:

Have you ever let go of something that in hindsight was the perfect thing for you?

....
....
....
....

Have you ever given up at the first sign of a struggle?

....
....
....

Sometimes it might be better to stick it out and see what comes of something rather than running away. Letting someone else's opinion change the course of your life is not smart.

IME MOMENT:
Decided to let go of a relationship that was getting stale, knowing that I had done what I had come to do (get Mark to attend University to follow his dreams) age 19

My first long term boyfriend Mark was quite literally gorgeous; he was the complete package, until he got boring…

I like to help people to achieve their dreams, its something that drives me forward. When I first met him, Mark had this dream to go to University to become a Sports and Science teacher, and so I encouraged him, I went to the University campus and collected the forms he needed to apply and filled them in with him. It was all very foreign to him and he was very self conscious, he didn't feel like he would get in and felt that he was "past it" as he would have to enter as a mature aged student (at the grand old age of 23). He was coming from the world's most boring job for a Rail company in London.

I didn't see any of his problems as obstacles and so I encouraged him regardless. As suspected, he got in and he was elated. I was happy that I had helped him to achieve his dream. Mark was a great student and was remarkably studious. We started University at the same time, but on different campuses and so we understandably led separate lives. When we did catch up all he wanted to do was stay home and watch movies. It wasn't what I wanted to do as I was keen to go out and do things and so we started to see less of each other.

So after an eighteen month long relationship it was time to part ways, especially after I quit Uni and started working in London, the dynamic was altered and going backwards was not an option. It was a hard decision as I really was very fond of him, he was my first "love" and my first sexual partner, but with travel on my mind and the rush of London in my veins hanging out in his mum and dads house in Welling was stunting my fun and it had to stop.

LESSON:
That life evolves, when it doesn't feel right change the scene or you'll stagnate. It feels good to help someone to achieve a dream. I guess I was meant to meet him to help him to apply and get into Uni. It changed his life and he enriched mine as a result. Win-Win.

Ask Yourself:

Have you ever been in a situation and it comes to a natural end?

....

....

....

Have you ever helped someone to fulfil one of their dreams?

....

....

....

Do you realise that life is an evolutionary process and all the life events are all part of the weaving of your amazing life tapestry.

Review of life to date
Life was about to take a very different path from anything I had ever known; I was totally ready for it. I didn't feel like I couldn't in any way shape or form and just took the bull by the horns. I had been on a journey of discovery and felt like I had started to find out whom I really was. The next few years would shape my future and I had no idea what was in store for me. But I was ripe.

Backpacker Angie arrives

IME MOMENT:
The era of working in London and meeting lots of travellers. Age 19

When I decided to leave Uni I started to work for a publishing company in Covent Garden, which literally changed my whole life. Dorling Kindersley was the Company and it was jam packed with Aussies, Kiwi's, South Africans and travellers of all types, I had found my home. For the first time I belonged, I was the outrageous one and I was the life of the party and I loved it.

Alcohol became my water, one-pound Pizza my fuel, 'Land Downunder' my anthem and Vic (an Aussie), my new best friend and we had so much fun, its makes me smile just writing about it. Yeah we would work, we did a good job too. We were production assistants (a kind way of saying "dogs bodies") and we thrived on it, we were answerable (to a point, not sure that anyone really cared as long as the tasks were complete) but our days were filled with sorting post, delivering stuff, checking production film, filling up libraries and essentially floating between buildings to catch up with our mates.

I'd be the one who helped to organise the company softball team, well not really oragnise much to do with the game at all, I'd be the one to go and collect everyone's beer money and then buy a slab of beer and take it to the park for pre and post training beers (I had my priorities straight). Lunch time was mostly spent in the Aussie pub drinking pints of beer and eating curly fries and so we'd go back to work with a nice little buzz happening and a mind full of cheek to dish out to the "lads". Oh the fun, and what trouble we got into. Bah hah!!!

Those 18 months feel like a time warp, it felt like it lasted forever - it was so much fun, I'm sure my liver cried every day. Vic and I would hang out most weekends without fail, sometimes opting to take off for the weekend to festivals or to places like the Black Mountains in Wales, just for an adventure. We'd have great conversations about a planet we invented called "Zetty", the planet was full of purple cows, the people were "Zettians" and were all very cool and it rained beer on Zetty. So naturally, Beerflavourrain became my email address for many years as I travelled. Such good times, I miss those days from time to time…

Working at DK led me to make the huge decision to go travelling to Australia & NZ for 18 months on my own. I was initially going to go with a friend, who also worked at DK, but she as luck would have it she "fell in love" (vomit) and reneged on the deal and so I carried on regardless. Little did I know that this would be the biggest decision of my life and one that would shape my world from that point forwards.

Those 18 months were my planning and saving months. I saved my heart out. I held down another job in the evenings in a bar in Blackheath where I had to wear a stupid kilt (One punter thought it was open invitation to put his grubby little mitts up my skirt, lets just say I was soon the only girl wearing jeans at work from that point forwards and he had an early night after being thrown out) and on the nights when I wasn't working, I would party hard.

At work on my desk I had an old parcel tube and on that tube I stuck all of the images of Australia and NZ and what I was planning to do. My friends would add more to it for me. It became known as the "Tat Tube" and it was like a vision board for me (I didn't even know what a "vision board" was at that point). See if you think about something so hard and focus on it everyday then it will happen, because thoughts become things.

I know my Mum and Dad supported my decision to travel, I'm not sure if they knew that it would mean that they would lose their 2nd born to the other side of the planet yet though…

LESSON:

If you have a dream, create a plan around it, literally visualise it and make it happen, regardless of what other people's plans and ideas are. It's your life – you have to live it for you, not anyone else.

Ask Yourself:

Do you remember the last time in your life when you were carefree and giddily happy?

....

....

Have you ever made plans that took a long time to come into fruition but enjoyed the process of waiting for it to happen? This is the gold dust of life.

....

....

....

Have you got a dream but are waiting for the perfect time for it to happen? Stop waiting – the time is now. Visualise it – try it – it works.

....

....

....

The process of planning and waiting for your next adventure is all part of the beauty of life, don't overlook the process because it should all be a huge part of how much you enjoy your "planned" experience. What I'm saying is don't wait to be happy, be happy in the moment, be happy now because plans change, never say I'll be happy when..... just enjoy each day. Life is better that way.

IME MOMENT:
The Melbourne Love connection that wasn't what I expected. Age 20

I did fall in love/lust whilst I was at DK. Damien was a security Guard and very handsome, no he was absolutely gorgeous. He was tall, dark and quite quiet (not like the confident being that I had morphed into) and he was Australian. I already had plans to go to Australia, and this increased the connection. As I'd make my mail rounds of the buildings I'd go into the building he was guarding and every time without fail he'd sing 'Angie' by the Rolling Stones to me. It made me swoon! I'd find reasons to deliver stuff to his building even if I didn't actually have very much at all. It's all a little teenage. It makes me laugh now.

The funny thing was that we danced around each other for months and never actually connected romantically. We were both aware that we liked each other, but he was painfully shy right up until his leaving party when he escorted me to the ATM to get some money out and then he kissed me. Talk about leaving it until the last minute. That's it, that's all we had and this filled my head for months. I wrote letters to him, which I snail mailed to Australia (this was before email was really popular) and waited patiently for his replies (which were few and far between - incidentally this killed me and should have been a red flag).

The day came to fly to Australia, we had arranged for my first stop to be Melbourne and I was to stay with Damian and his Brother and Sister in Law. They were to meet me at the airport and it was going to be magnificent...

Now as we can all see, my imagination is brilliant and it conjured up all sorts of scenarios about this situation, none of which came true. (I must stop believing my own illusions).

I still was in that "Love" stage with Damian, I'm not sure he ever entered it with me and I'm 100% sure he regretted even answering my letters. Everything was awkward, we didn't know each other and neither of us were open enough to smooth out the wrinkles. He was really into Cricket, Surfing and being a boy and was actually far more subdued than I ever imagined. For a few months we tried to make it work, then I decided to go travelling up the east coast of Australia for 6 weeks on my own. I stayed with an old friend from London up in Cairns, which was fun. In that time, I fitted in things like White Water Rafting, Skydiving, Great Barrier Reef trips, foam parties, beer drinking competitions, and a whole heap more. It was the break we needed to ultimately decide that this was not a path either of us wanted to walk down for long. 3 days before my 21st Birthday we decided that I'd move out, so my 21st birthday was spent looking for somewhere else to live. I felt utterly defeated, sad and cheated of what my head had created. Damian did try and make up with me a few months later but I was past it and really happy to just let that go. (I'm evolving)

LESSON:
See reality, making shit up in your head is not the answer. Expecting reality to be a direct mirror of your dreams and expectations is a recipe for disappointment and ultimate failure.

Ask Yourself:

When was the last time you made up a scenario in your head and expected real life to pan out exactly as you imagined?

....

....

....

Have you ever pursued someone who was not really responding but pushed the envelope anyway? How'd that work out for you?

....

....

....

IME MOMENT:
My Travelling days

I spent 18 months working my way around Australia & NZ. This was the most cathartic experience of my life to this point. Breaking free of the student and worker chains was so good for me. Having no one to impress was also good for me. I've spent far too much of my life worrying about what other people felt, wanted, expected of me. Having all of my worldly possessions in one bag on my back made me feel so very free and liberated. It still does. Every time I don the backpack I'm back into backpacker Angie mode and I love it!

Some of my fondest memories of travelling are all when I am in nature.
I guess it's where I'm happiest, I feel so energised from the trees. Funny that when I was a kid I always used to say to my family "I want to be a tree" – its true, I do.. Still – haha

My days as backpacker Angie were free, liberating, lonely at times, but more than anything they were fun. I worked my way around Australia & NZ and met so many people. However whilst I worked my way around, I still felt like I wasn't as cool as some of the other backpackers. I wonder if they felt that way too?

I would work in pubs mostly, because I had done a lot of bar work in the UK and I knew that this way I would meet people and I'd create a circle of misfit mates. It worked; I had an absolute ball (all except at the topless bar in the suburbs of Perth that I worked in as a non topless waitress - that was just odd). I also worked in offices too, and sometimes I did both. Having no one to answer to or have to go home to was good, so I just pleased myself.

There was a period of time over in Perth in Western Australia where I felt so free, so happy and like I was growing up and I could literally feel it. Working in an office during the day and in a very popular nightspot 4 evenings a week took up a whole bunch of time, but once I'd earned enough cash to travel again I was gone. First stop The Pinnacles during the Wild Flower Season. I've never seen so much beauty and experienced such serenity. I remember climbing to the top of a rocky area and surveying the land that was laid out bare for me to take in. The only thing that spoilt this moment was that my shoes absolutely stunk – guess I should have worn socks..

In this space I felt like I was part of the scene, when the wind swirled around me I felt like I blended in, like I belonged. The sun beat down on my fair skin and warmed my soul, my face was relaxed as my mouth smiled acknowledging the peace I felt. There are times in your life when you feel like you are in your true essence. This is one of them for me and I wasn't doing anything to be in that space, just being open, enjoying nature and letting go. It's a space I yearn for these days as my hectic life blows like a tornado.

I was hooked on Australia, an affliction that will stay with me for the rest of time.

The soundtrack of my travelling days was epitomized by Crowded House and their 'Distant Sun' tune, the lyrics "still so young to travel so far, old enough to know who you are, wise enough to carry the scars, without any pain, there's no one to blame" sit with me to this day and cast me straight back into backpacker Angie days every time I hear it. Happy days!

LESSON:
Work hard, but find the serenity too. In the silence your being will shine. Travelling is so good for you; the world is an incredible place – go look at it.

Ask Yourself:

What makes you feel free and liberated?

....

....

Can you think back and remember where your fondest memories are located?

....

....

Why do you sometimes think that you're not enough and not cool enough?

....

....

Where do you find your serenity and how often do you go there?

....

....

When was the last time you did something you've never done before or explored a new place, it's liberating – go!

IME MOMENT:
To pursue a relationship with Duncan at age 22. Which led me to Bournemouth to study again, then travel around the world again. Age 25

After my Australia / NZ trip I came back to London to settle back into life in the UK. I quickly secured a job with a high-end textile company that manufactured upholstery & drapery fabrics. It was there that I met Duncan. He worked on one side of London in the warehouse and I worked at Head Office in the posh suburbs with the Marketing team.

A whole bunch of us were taken over to the warehouse to do a tour of the facility and that's when I saw him. He was very tall, long dark hair, goatie beard and big blue eyes; he was incredible to look at and a South African so "exotic". Apparently, however he was a bit of an obnoxious git (which I had not experienced and so I reserved judgment on that). He was also married, but separated. Anyway he and his wife filed for divorce and Duncan and I started what would be a long 4-year relationship that would have its up and downs.

Those first 6 months were amazing, we were head over heels in love with each other, we literally couldn't get enough of each other. But like most things as time passes, so too does an infatuation.

I wanted to go back to Uni and see if I could obtain a degree (that I still coveted the idea of), so we packed up our separate lives in London and moved to Bournemouth so I could attend the Art School that I had gained a place at. We bought a flat instead of renting – it seemed so silly to rent when you could essentially use the same money as a savings plan in property. We were in that "forever" stage of our lives and we never envisaged not being together, so it felt right.

Duncan decided that he would also attend Uni, which really annoyed me as he already had several degrees and had no interest in art whatsoever. I knew it was so he could keep an eye on me. He ended up just doing a part time course and once he realised that there was no threat he left me to my own devices. God it annoyed me though, to not feel trusted. That was the start of the inkling that this was not right for me.

After the first year of the course concluded Duncan felt the urge to go travelling, my course was annoyingly changing from a 3D Design course that focused on installation and furniture into a Small Product course, I lobbied against this profusely, but nothing changed and so instead of pursuing a degree that I had no interest in, I decided yet again to withdraw from University.

We got jobs at a big American Bank that was based in Bournemouth for a while to save up some cash. We sold the flat and took off for a 6-month tour of the world. It was a good trip, but it would have been better solo, as Duncan seemed to be the captain of the ship and anywhere I had ever been before was completely off limits! It was "my way or the highway" with him, which was so unattractive and highly irritating. Not that I wanted to retrace my steps, but if I mentioned my previous travel experiences he would get the shits and literally tell me off, so I stopped talking about my travels and to be honest I haven't really ever told anyone much since. I do feel like people who haven't travelled aren't interested in the tales from those who have seen the world. Its almost like they are jealous of your adventures.

I gave up talking about these times a long time ago. So as I write this book it seems like I don't pay my travelling days much homage. They were my growth days, my soul finding and character-building stage of life to date. If I hadn't gone, I'd be a completely different person – so they are part of me, just locked up (a little).

During Duncan and my travels, we went to China, Hong Kong, Thailand, Cambodia, Bali, some islands around Indonesia (the Gili Islands), Australia, NZ, Rarotonga, BoraBora, Tahiti, Hawaii, LA, St Luis OBispo, New York and

Home to London. It was a great trip, we met so many amazing people, immersed ourselves into various cultures.

We did have a couple of amazing learning experiences I want to share before I end this section of my life because the message is powerful and the experiences were memorable.

Here's a funny story from this trip

DOG NOT DUCK - CHINA
On this trip we learnt all about the art of communication and developing listening skills in the funniest /most horrific way possible.

After Being in China for a month as our first stop, the next location was Hong Kong. We arrived in the early hours of the morning and whilst still donning the 65litre back pack we were wandering around the streets looking for something to eat before we checked into the worst hotel in the history of the planet (a converted toilet complete with tiles on all walls, no windows and the most uncomfortable bed on earth on the 25th floor of a high rise tower) Welcome to the Chunking Mansions – far out, its one to remember. It's known as the Ghetto of Hong Kong – this we found out afterwards.

Anyway, we were hungry and so still wandering around the streets, we were stopped by a slim, short Chinese man who appeared to be early twenties and very enthused to suddenly meet two English speaking travellers on the street. He was studying English at the University and had found two willing victims to practice on. We were happy to chat to him, it was why we had travelled to these places, to immerse ourselves into the culture.

I mentioned that we were hungry and searching for a place to eat. He was so excited and said that he knew just the place, his friend owned a café around the corner. Brilliant – so off we all walked. It wasn't quite around the corner, but we did get there. By the time we got there I was starving; the menu however was all in Chinese as it was a local café, not one that was ever frequented by westerners and travellers. We were treated like royalty. I think all 4 staff members waited on us (there was no one else in the café – red flag 1).

The set up was a little unorthodox, the tables were low to the ground, made of milk crates, the seats were those low white plastic seats you have in the garden, but they were old and brittle so you kind of sat down and stayed still. (red flag 2)

The Chinese man (forgive me I cannot remember his name) said that as we did not understand the menu, if it was OK, he would order for us. We agreed, as our bellies rumbled.

The tea was served, which looked like brown muddy sticks in water and unfortunately tasted like it too, but we were in polite mode...

The first dish came out, it was a type of meat on a bed of cauliflower, and we tucked in. It looked like fish and tasted more like chicken, except a bit tougher. The next dish came out which looked like sweet and sour duck on rice, as it was a little oiler than chicken. Whatever, we were hungry.

Then the chap started to speak, he was telling us that the first dish was something of a delicacy in the area, it was a "five step" snake. OK so we had just eaten Snake. I asked him why "five step"; he said that it was because if this snake bites you – you take five steps and you are dead. He said that only the best chefs can prepare it, as we sat in this dirty back water café in Hong Kong, maybe I should have been worried. He said that the snakes were kept on site and killed to order, so this wriggling dude has just met his maker for us. I asked him if the ducks (the meat in the other dish) were also kept out the back. Fair question right!

His response was (think in a Chinese accent) "Duck, no, no not Duck..... DOG!!!!
He tried to make it better by saying, "its OK, it was only a small one"...
As the colour drained from my face, the realisation hit me that I had just consumed puppy!!!!

LESSON:
Maybe ask questions before you eat. This is one of those stories that will always be funny, mortifyingly funny and will etch into my head from now until I die. How important is communication.

Another Story

INTERROGATION ON THE MOUNTAIN WITH NINJAS
Another memorable event that took place in China was visiting the Shaolin Monastery. Duncan was really into Martial Arts and liked the Buddhist values and had a passion to visit these amazing ninja's and see them training on the mountain, so we went.

The train journey out there was very interesting and an eye opener to say the least. The train was more like a cattle truck with a roof and sides, it was crammed full of Chinese locals and their families or all of their worldly possessions.

The passengers knew that this was going to be a long and slow journey to their destinations and they were prepared (we in comparison – weren't). They got their camping stoves out and all their ingredients and right there in the middle of the aisle they all started cooking up a storm.

We sat next to a family whose teenage daughter had never seen a Walkman so for the duration of the trip she wore my Walkman and sang songs she had never heard. Not sure if Alannis Morisette ever took off in China – but this young girl seemed to like her entire album.

We were fed by this family and taught some of the language; they were so kind to us. They had so little and we "Western people had so much" yet they were the ones giving to us. It touched my heart that day and I'll always remember that train journey with fondness.

We disembarked the train and took a local bus up the mountain to the temple, backpacks in tow. We had not booked accommodation as we had intended to camp.

We spent the day with the monks at the temple watching them train, doing meditations with them and being shown around their monastery – they were so accommodating to us and were really happy to have people come to learn about their ways. The monk we were with for most of the time gave us Jade Buddha bracelets at the end of the day for us to remember him by. I'll never forget him, but mostly because he probably saved our skin later that night.

We walked out of the monastery and made our way up the mountain and found a clearing where we thought it was a good spot to make camp, we set up the tent and started cooking our food on the little gas stove we had with us. Just then, we heard a heap of noise, car doors shutting, footsteps pounding over in our direction and several Police officers stood (armed) with torches shining at us. We silently shit ourselves....

They demanded to see our Passports and interrogated us as to why we were there. We told them that we had been to the Shaolin Monastery and that we were just staying overnight and heading off first thing. They would have none of it, apparently the Mountain was Sacred and we were not allowed to camp there without permission from the Shaolin Monks themselves.

Then out of the trees a small monk appeared, the same monk we had spent the day with. He calmed the Police officers down and told them that we were invited to camp there at his invitation for one night only. Our Passports were thrust back at us and we were given a warning never to do this again. I don't think I'll ever do it again, rest assured!

The monk stayed with us until the Police had left, we chatted for a while, he pressed his palms together, bowed and left.

I was so grateful for this monk and his intuition to come and seek out what the commotion was about.

The funny thing was that I had a bad feeling about camping there, I had expressed my concerns to Duncan but he had poo pooed me off and told me to chill out that it'd be fine, well I should have listened to my intuition. However in hindsight it taught me that even complete strangers are willing to put themselves out to help others. It taught me to be grateful and it taught me to listen to myself more.

Ask Yourself

When was the last time that you had bad feeling about what might happen and then something happens and you know you should have listened to yourself?

....

....

....

Have you ever met anyone who has stuck their neck out for you? Be grateful these people are rare. Maybe its time to pay that forward?

....

....

....

This trip had afforded us a lot of learning experiences but this relationship was never going to last. Something changed in Duncan and when we came back to Bournemouth he wanted to become this darker individual. He was always into Death Metal, which I hated with a passion but tolerated (you cannot like everything the other does), but he came back with this idea of turning into a fully blown Goth and wanted to weave a bird's nest into his hair and dye it blue (odd). I wasn't into it at all. It had to stop. His darkness and controlling nature made me fear him, I hated that feeling. I never want to feel like I cannot be myself or do the things that are important to me ever again.

One weekend we went to a friend's house for a BBQ, their house was packed with people, some we knew and some we didn't. We had just adopted two kittens and they were very young. Duncan and I had been drifting apart for a while and so we led separate lives almost, I got a great job with another Textile company and he went back to the Bank which I think suited both of us. Anyway I left him at the party to go and feed the kittens (I'm sure they could have waited, I just needed an out) so I left him with a very attractive girl who was totally into him and let them get on with the initial meeting, which was obviously taking place.

Three weeks later I found a 3-page love sonnet on the shared computer we used at home, it was written to the girl he had met at the party. Relief swept over me like a tsunami and I knew that this was my chance to get out. On our way to the supermarket I casually (to my credit) brought the poem up and watched as the colour drained out of his face and he started to stutter and make excuses. I was very calm and collected because I knew this was my chance. He had always said to me that if I ever left him, he would kill me and so I was quite literally scared of him. This was perfect as it was not my fault (directly). I told him I wanted to move out so I could have some space. That space was always going to be a forever situation (much to his dismay) and I was free. Walking home, 'The Eye of the Tiger' played in my head, I felt like I won a major battle an got out unscathed...

It's funny having those feelings about someone that you were once so very much into. It goes to show you that people change and the honeymoon period is a very real thing.

LESSON:
Trust your gut, red flags appear for a reason. Never fear another human, like I found out – the ones to fear are always the weakest because they think that threats and power are the way to retain control.

Ask Yourself:

Have you ever been in a relationship where you were not the captain of the ship and disliked it?

....

....

....

....

Have you ever been scared of another human, if so what did you do about it?

....

....

....

....

Marriage, Dogs & Business & Kids...

IME MOMENT:
To move to the other side of the world to give into the magnetic pull that Australia had on me. Age 26

After leaving Duncan and his controlling ways. I spent 6 months living alone in a bedsit on the outskirts of Bournemouth. At times I was lonely, at times I was fine. I'd never really lived completely alone before as I'd always had flat mates. This was good for me. Duncan tried to weasel his way back in and I shut him out completely. It felt right, mean but right. I could have caved and gone back, but I'd just be going backwards and that makes no sense at all. So I met some new friends and planned another trip to Australia to see an old friend who I'd met working in London. I kind of liked my little hovel, it was small and dark and had a pull down bed, but it was clean and practical. I'd make more food than I needed and freeze some so I had food to eat when I couldn't be bothered to cook.

I remember making my own garlic bread and living on that more often than not. I cycled everywhere in those days and so shopping was limited as it was all about what I could fit into my backpack. I remember sitting in my little hole listening to Fleetwood Mac (Mums influence) singing about going your own way, thinking that this was so very true and that I really had gone my own way. I was happy and felt free.

During the time that I lived on my own, the Textile Company I was working for was bought out by a larger company and they asked me to move to East Sussex with them to be part of a larger marketing department. I decided that if I was going to move anywhere that I was going to move to Australia, not to the middle of England to lead the world's most boring existence. So I turned my already planned trip into a business trip and lined up three job interviews. I attended all three interviews, and promptly got offered three jobs, I took the best one and 5 weeks later I immigrated to Australia on my own with just my backpack. Again, in heaven in my own space, living the dream.

My Mum and Dad were now all too aware that Australia has managed to pull me back. I know it broke their hearts to watch me immigrate, but I do know that they now understand my reason to choose this life and I admire their bravery for letting me go.

Before I left my sister and I had words, she questioned why I was going away again. She was married and had just had their first child 2 days before I departed for Australia for good. I guess she was angry at me for bowing out of family life. I have a distinct memory of a conversation that has stayed with me. As she disputed my arrangements I said to her "don't you think I want what you have" meaning a husband, a home and a family. It was the first time that I'd really ever voiced that actually maybe I would like those things. I think it also took me by surprise. Today I have the husband, the house, the kids, the dogs, and the responsibility and sometimes on those days when the tantrums are a full capacity and everything is hectic and crazy I sometimes don't believe my initial statement... Just sometimes...

When I got to Australia the third time round, I stayed at an old pilot friend's house. He was best mates with Damian - the boy I fell in love with in Melbourne all those years ago. He wasn't home so I essentially got to use him apartment for nix while I found my feet and got accommodation sorted.

The first (and last) apartment I went to see was in Randwick, it was in the right location, close enough for me to cycle to my new job and close enough to Coogee (the party area I knew I'd love). Essentially I couldn't be bothered to look harder. The room was musty, small and the unit was grubby and filled with cockroaches, but I took it. It was alright, it was cheap and I never intended to spend much time in it anyway. I'd only met one of the housemates, the other one was off skiing and so I had no idea what to expect. I was told that he was a carpenter though. One box immediately got ticked and as Live said ' "Lightening Crashes' and a new chapter was born...

LESSON:
Seek out your dreams; make them a reality because no one is going to do this for you. Choose the path less travelled – it's more interesting
Be careful what you wish for – you might just get it...

Ask Yourself:

Have you ever taken a massive leap of faith without knowing what the consequences would be?

....

....

Have you ever left all of your family and friends on the other side of the planet in search of something you cannot describe?

....

....

Do you have big dreams and are sitting on the fence waiting for someone to tell you to do it or not? You decide – get on with it.

....

....

IME MOMENT:
Met Kev 3 days after landing (Tall, dark haired carpenter with a nice bum) and decided to go with the flow and let go of a potential relationship that was unlikely to ever take shape. Age 26

The walk from the bus with my backpack had been a hot one. Randwick has a few hills. I clambered my way up the dank dark staircase to the cream, paint flecked front door of the unit I would call home for a short time. I knocked on the door and was greeted by Lisa, the female flatmate I had previously met. As I walked in the front door of the unit with my backpack on, fleece jacket, jeans and Blundstones, I met the other flatmate. It was Kev, (little did I know) - my now husband...

He was a tall, dark haired man with a big smile on his face and a twinkle in his eye. From the first moment he was humourous and the banter started immediately.

Standing there with all my worldly possessions on my back I knew I needed to break the ice. So I offered to go and get some beers from the bottle-shop not realising it was a good 1.5kms walk there and back (remember Randwick is hilly). Kev had hurt his shoulder skiing and also he was injured so I went alone. Anyway I went, bought a case, chucked it on my shoulder and walked back. This apparently impressed Kev no end, although to this day he still complains about the type of beer I bought (the kind I liked).

We decided to go out for the night as a group, much to Kev's disgust. I don't think he had hung out with his other flat mate much. I pushed the point and also pushed to let Lisa the other flatmate choose where we would go. This was Kev's first experience with compromise for me – I now look back and deep belly laugh at this!

It was fair to say that where Lisa chose to go was crap, her local pub, filled to the brim with bogans (people wearing checked shirts, with no or few teeth, a few days from their last decent shower, with more grease in their hair than you need to fry chips). As ACDC and WhiteSnake pump out of the Wurlitzer, Kev and I started to get on (we appeared to be the only non bogans in the joint, so process of elimination was short).

After a few too many beers, we all went over to the local nightclub – Randiwicks (equally as bad as the pub - the name should have given it away) to hang out with the Bogans some more (God only knows why I pushed this point- anyway...). We could have ended up down The Coogee Bay Hotel listening to better live music, hanging out with our own kind of tribe, but then Kev and I would not have connected and knowing him now, he would have ended up flirting with all the other girls and I'd end up in the corner trapped by some old weirdo in a grey suit (it always seems to happen to me – no idea why). So anyway, we hooked up on the first night (such a classy chick). That's me though, jump in – balls and all.

We had a great night even amongst the Bogans and we started to hang out more. I resisted at first as I had my heart set on catching up with an Aussie guy I'd met in Bournemouth (UK). That never eventuated – Kev saw to that. I could have been living in Tarthra by now possibly as a bit of a hippie with an airline mechanic. That's not the way life went and I'm alright with that.

We would spend a lot of time in Coogee over the coming years listening to live music which invariably always included renditions of Cold Chisel Classics like 'Khe Sahn' and drinking far too much beer, but those times were fun, good and made us connect on an even ground we otherwise might not have found.

LESSON:
Go with the flow – good things can come of it.

Ask Yourself:

Have you ever gone out of your way to fit in?

....

....

....

Have you ever tried to be inclusive of everyone even if it means going somewhere or doing something that you didn't really want to?

....

....

....

When was the last time you relaxed a bit and let things happen?

....

....

....

IME MOMENT:
To give Kev and I the best chance but surrendering and letting destiny take place hoping it was the right thing to do. Age 27

We didn't hit it off as smoothly as you might think for two people who are now married with kids. In fact, when I first started getting to know Kev, I didn't like him much and I had the airline mechanic floating around in my head. I made it quite clear to Kev, that I wasn't impressed with some of his traits and much to my surprise he made an enormous effort and changed – for me. I'd like to state that I never once told him he needed to change, he decided that he wanted to change and that I would be the catalyst to help him make the leap. I highly commend him for this and to this day, he has kept it up!

So I let my guard down and let go of a love interest that would never happen and I (slowly) let him in. We started to officially date, we already lived together as flat mates but the requirement for two rooms soon became void and so we moved out together to another share house into one room. We both had ok wages coming in and so in those days we had a very free and carefree existence in Sydney, working, partying, dating and enjoying ourselves with a healthy disposable income. I remember having enough of a disposable income to be comfortable buying what we now consider "expensive" wine just for quaffing. It's incredible to think that in one year we managed to save $28K to go overseas to the UK for 6 weeks without really trying that hard. Those were the days...

One weekend we went down the coast to the Sussex Inlet where Kev's parents had a caravan. It was a lovely peaceful spot and I felt chilled and happy there. We went out to the local pub on the Saturday night and on the way back after several beverages (FYI Kev to this date thinks that the word several means seven – I have tried to educate him over the years – to no avail, it was definitely more than seven drinks), he asked me to marry him. I said tentatively yes, but told him that he needed to ask me properly when we had not been out drinking. He seemed happy with that and took it as a yes anyway.

We had booked a trip to the UK at the end of our first year together so he could meet my family in Kent and I could meet his extended family up north in Widnes. We took a 6-week break, which was huge and if I'm honest a little too long. You can only eat so many bacon sandwiches.

As a student, I used to live in Bournemouth so we took a trip back there to go and see some of my old mates and visit some old haunts. It was during this part of the trip that he officially proposed to me. We were staying in The Langtry Manor Hotel that was built by King Edward VII in the late 1800's. It was in the Kings bedroom in-front of a huge fireplace, that Kev stood suited and booted (and looking very sharp) holding a glass of champagne that he asked me to be Mrs. Hammond. We are now 13 years into marriage and have two little beasts running around and so you can guess how it's worked out.

LESSON:
Take a chance, make sure you are honest with people, see the best in people and let things happen once in a while instead of trying to control situations. If I had not let my guard down, we would not be together today and Kev would not have even wanted to change his behaviours. People can change but they have to want to, you cannot change someone, it's not how it works.

Ask Yourself:

Can you remember the last time you took a chance on something that made a huge difference in your life?

....

....

Do you see the best in people and if not why?

....

....

Do you try to change people and if so why?

....

....

Note about the rest of this book
Life was getting "serious", I wasn't "Backpacker Angie" anymore as much as I fought that, I had been part of a couple for a few years now and we had just moved to another State to "settle down". It's a little scary looking back but I took it all in my stride. Now we had responsibility, a house with a garden, we were about to get pets, get married, then a little while later we were looking at going into major league debt with a mortgage. Then I suppose at some point the stomp of crazy Hammond children hooves would arrive. (Our children wouldn't be pitter patterers...). There comes a time in a woman's life when all of this stuff happens and you suddenly find yourself all grown up. Well fuck me, I guess this was it!

IME MOMENT:
To move to Brisbane and start our lives as a family unit Age 28

Living in Sydney was ridiculously expensive especially if you wanted to own property and a car. Most of the time we were having an absolute ball drinking away any funds we earned, but that life (insanely) was also getting a little boring, I was getting a bit fed up and felt left out and the party life was getting monotonous. Perhaps I was losing my mind (looking back, surely this must have been the case, because these days we cannot escape unless we pay someone an inordinate amount of money to look after our cherubs and it negates the point of going out, then when we are out we are tired by 10:30pm – FFS)...

It was in Sydney that Garnish (my now business) was first born. I used to make greeting cards and beaded necklaces. Kev helped me to set up my very first market stall at the Bondi markets. It was a great day, I was so nervous initially, it was a little rainy that day, but it turned out ok and I sold some stock. The craft side of the business didn't last long though and I had stock of those cards for years afterwards. However what I remember from this time is the invaluable support that Kev gave to me during this time. He knew I wanted to do something of my own and he helped me in so many ways to achieve this. I was feeling discontented with work and felt like I didn't really fit in very well (It is a common thread in my life). I had a good job but not something I could see myself doing forever. Things felt like they were starting to shift, that itch started to become irritable.

At the time I was also getting some horrible stomach issues which led to a series of tests and a laparoscopy, uncovering the fact that they thought I had "Mild IBS" which is technical speak for "Miss Callan, we actually have no fucking clue what is wrong with your gut so we are giving it a label and you can just stop eating wheat". I still have gut issues to this day. It started to stress me out. This is the first time the cracks started to appear in my demeanour and the black dog came for a short visit. Looking back, I think I am just a stress head and stress causes my gut issues, I overthink too much and I'm really good at making shit up in my head.

I guess the reason for being a bit fed up was a combination of work woes, the need to be doing something myself and because Kev had a heap of "footy" mates who he hung out with a fair bit, I felt a tad alone. I had our flat mate and a few other cool chick mates but again (it's getting boring) I never really felt like I fitted in, they were awesome girls though and we still keep in contact, I've no idea why I felt so alienated - it's something I was fabricating myself. Perhaps I self sabotage a lot. I remember feeling like the odd one out, like I was in the way, like I didn't belong. Sometimes I felt like if I organised a night out I shouldn't, because it didn't involve Kev. I still have this problem today.

I was never very good at making friends. All of Kev's mates had girlfriends, none of whom I felt like I resonated with very well at the time (I'm actually fine with them now when we go back to Sydney and catch up – but anyway that was me in my mid twenties) and so I disassociated myself with them. I felt like an outsider in my own life and felt incapable of "joining in" for some stupid reason. I sowed the first seeds of resentment.

Kev and I discussed that perhaps it was time to change and settle down a bit and stop "partying so much". (Pass me the gun, I'll put myself out of my own misery – idiot!) But that is what happened. My internal clock was telling me it was time to "slow down, settle down and grow wider hips".

We both wanted to have kids, dogs, a house and all that; we'd been speaking about it for ages. Every time we would see people walking their dogs in Sydney I'd stop to pat the dog, I never quite got to the "I need to pat the baby" stage – which is probably good as I might have been arrested for being odd. Plus I've never been very maternal.

However property prices were so hideous in Sydney it was unachievable to start this idyllic lifestyle we both envisaged there and so on a whim Kev suggested that we move to Queensland to start our lives together. We knew we would never be able to afford a house in Sydney and so Kev and his best mate Clarkey flew up to Brisbane to do a rekkie on the area, he secured us a rental property and without me having seen the place, (I've never really cared much for status and appearances so whatever he thought I knew would be fine) we packed up our lives in Sydney and drove our small white Ford Laser (Flo) up to Brisbane. I have to commend Kev here for leaving his entire life behind and taking me to another State to try and give me the life I wanted and help me to stop stressing out. He still supports me in this way to this day (even through all the shit times)

The new house was huge; we had gone from a 2-bed unit in Coogee with a shared laundry to a 4-bedroom house with a garden overnight. We were really pleased with our life change and settled in quickly. In fact, we had unpacked in the space of a day or two and then went out to buy some more furniture to fill the space up because we literally didn't have enough to fill this vast house.

The decision to move and the actual move was all done inside 5 weeks. We are definitely the kind of people who make quick decisions and then act upon them. Life still runs at that pace.

LESSON:
If you want something be prepared to change everything to get it. Change is good, it means you are progressing. See everything as a positive and it will be just that. We love living in QLD, (Kev might argue all apart from 'State of Origin' time). It's now home and we wouldn't change that initial decision for the world.

Ask Yourself:

Have you ever had a huge goal, but to obtain it meant that everything you knew would have to change?

Are you resistant to change and if so why?

What is your next massive goal and how do you intend to make it happen?

....

....

....

....

....

IME MOMENT:
To bring Harvey into our lives – our first fur child age 28

We always knew that we wanted a dog. I had always wanted a Chocolate Labrador and so that is exactly what we got. Kev single handedly located a breeder and ordered him when we were in Sydney as a surprise for me (I was soooo excited). So then when we moved to QLD and he was ready all we had to do was collect him. We were first to order and so we got to pick the first pup from the litter. Arriving at the regional airport in Brisbane (our collection point) I was really nervous and excited. Being first in line, we scanned the cages and saw him. His big amber coloured eyes, velvet ears and big chubby wobbly legs made me fall in love instantly. We chose the biggest boxiest headed pup of the lot. He was gorgeous. I'm still in love to this day even though that sadly he has now passed away from Nasal Cancer (June 17th 2016) but my love for him will never fade, I do miss my Harvey.

Harvey was naughty, he would chew up the plants in the garden, he chewed up his beds (plural), we have photos of white fluffy filling strewn across the garden, he chewed up boxes that came by courier (I worked from home at that stage). Harvey chewed up anything he could find including plucking my favourite top off of the line and eating the straps.

He would lay underneath our Queen sized bed - right in the middle so neither of us could physically reach him and he would sit there and wag his tail laughing at us (I have photographic evidence of this). He would poo on the very cream rug we had, he would run away to go and see the horses at the end of the road whom he thought wanted to play (they really didn't).

He would wrap himself around Kev's head at night so they would both wake up sweating. He would poo in the back of the Ute every single time we took him out to the creek for a run, which was foul. He ate a length of rope once and was struggling to pass it, so I found myself tugging on this rope that was hanging out of his butt and pulling the poo covered rope free from his intestine – now that WAS disgusting! Looking back at all of these naughty doggie things, it was so funny, just like watching your first child do crazy things.

Harvey was gentle and crazy, his ears felt like velvet and he had a certain doggy smell that was distinctly his. The love you have for a pet is incredible, dogs are amazing creatures, they are unconditionally yours, they have no questions, no criticisms, just love and for that, I loved him back – unconditionally. (Poo rope n 'all)

Harvey was our first fur child. 12 years on and at the end of his life, he was much slower and older and had a cancer tumor in his nose. I knew for some time that he would not be long for this world and it literally broke my heart. I know that we gave him the best life he could have wished for and I am grateful for every second we have had with him.

Even till his last days he would try to escape down the hill to go and get into the creek, but by then we were faster than him and he'd get captured. He loved to swim, we'd take him whenever we could to the beach where it wasn't so rough and let him chase sticks into the water and them wrestle them off of Frankie our other dog and his best mate. God I miss him, his smell, his eyes and the way he'd look at me and just make my heart melt. I had a very special bond with Harvey and I'm not sure why, but I'd like to think that he has been my guardian as a dog for many existences and so if this is true, I'll see him in my next incarnation I'm sure. I have a song by Madness playing in my head as I write this, it's a song from childhood but it says it all – It Must be Love – because it was and it still is. Miss you mate. X

LESSON:
To unconditionally love someone is monumental. Animals are the best, they de stress you, they love you back and they make you laugh. Take the time to love them for they are not here for as long as us humans.

Ask Yourself:

Have you ever loved something unconditionally, so completely, so purely?

Have you ever felt the love of an animal?

Have you ever experienced the pain when your best mate goes to the other side?

To Love is to live, I would not have changed a thing with Harvey (apart from perhaps stopping him from getting cancer if I could).

IME MOMENT:
To bring Frankie into the fold – our second fur child age 29
Harvey needed a friend, so to end the constant chewing and destroying events that were almost daily happenings, we decided to get Harvey a mate.

One day we were on our way out to buy a new computer for my home business I was about to start up and we drove down the road past the RSPCA pound. Kev suggested that we go in to say hi to the puppies, I love puppies and it was something I'd never say no to, so we did and that was where we found the naughtiest puppy wagging her crazy little tail. She had come from a stray litter, her mum had given birth to her litter in the bushes of a park and someone had brought the family in to be looked after. She was one of the only ones left and so we decided that this was Harvey's new mate. They were inseparable.

Frankie was the female version of Harvey, she was a red cattle cross (we are still not sure what she is crossed with). Frankie was so cheeky, so funny. As soon as she arrived, she immediately knew her place in the pecking order and fitted into our little family perfectly. She would jump on him and he'd just let her. She would run around and yap at him. I'm sure they conspired to tear their beds up together. Harvey would drag them out into the garden and they would both just destroy them when we were both out of the house.

So our family started to grow, two naughty puppies certainly made the house brighter and livelier, also slightly more chewed and slobbered on.

Our responsibilities doubled but we loved it. We didn't go out so much these days just enjoyed spending time at home, in the garden and with the fur kids. It was a far cry from our drunken debauchery days of life in Coogee.

Sadly Frankie passed away at age 13 at home peacefully one morning not so long ago as we were about to leave for an overseas trip to Japan. She was a beautiful soul, who we all miss dearly.

LESSON:
It's important to have friends, and to recognise what another being needs over your own needs. Harvey needed a friend, so he got one.

Ask Yourself:

Do you have a friend who is everything to you, and do you know what they need from you?

IME MOMENT:
To change my perspective about Sales people by getting outside of my comfort zone aged 29

I used to be allergic to salespeople, almost as allergic as I still am to shopping malls now... They made me shudder, like shopping malls make me shudder today...

I had been working for a textile company since I landed in Australia. When I moved to Brisbane they kindly allowed me to continue to work for them but from my home base and use the Brisbane showroom as my point of contact. Then the company re structured and they moved all admin and marketing over to NZ. They did ask me to go over and manage the sampling from NZ but I had moved to Australia and so I politely declined. Kev and I had secured a defacto visa by then and so I was free to leave and obtain another job.

Unpacking | 91

I started working for a commercial furniture company as a sales rep, Kev was already working for this company and he could see that I'd be good at the role, so he encouraged me and set me up with an interview. I got the job.

Now here's the thing... I had an inherent dislike for sales people. After working in the high-end textile industry for around 8 years I had been so used to sales people (invariably women) who wore too much make up, too much perfume, and swanned around drinking coffee saying "daahhhling" and air kissing far too much. They annoyed the absolute crap out of me and so I chose to essentially ignore them, service their sampling and marketing needs and not engage with them and their fakeness.

As I am an evolving creature, the fact that I didn't like these people much annoyed me. It was more likely my problem. The way I see it is that we are sent lessons in this life. My lesson was to recognise that I was lacking in confidence and acceptance of this breed of people and to establish that I did not need to be anything other than who I am to thrive in a similar role. So I did something that has pretty much changed the shape of my life to date. Instead of rebelling against salespeople, I became one of them. I went out and got a job in sales, completely outside of my comfort zone. I had to learn how to sell and what to do with "customers". Luckily I had a good teacher and I was taken under the wing of one of the directors for the first few months. I quickly got the hang of it.

Selling Commercial Furniture is so far removed from selling fabric to end-users. Firstly you deal with the business that is buying the product for a project (so there is no emotional reason behind the purchase, it's a purely business transaction). The designers and architects had already worked out what they wanted and so we were just meeting the brief. We just needed to be front of mind and we did this by ensuring that the product catalogues were always up-to-date and that the client was happy. This taught me that there were two types of customers. End Consumers and B2B.

This understanding about how businesses worked helped me to think about my future differently and helped me to get over my judgmental behaviour towards other people I didn't really understand. Most of the time we rebel against what we don't understand because change is harder than anything.

I still hate fake women who air kiss and talk incessantly about shite, but I'd say that most normal humans without botox implanted in their eyebrows and lips would...

LESSON:
Having an inherent dislike for something just highlights your own faults. To literally get over these barriers you need to get outside of your comfort zone and throw yourself into an area that makes you feel uncomfortable. You'll soon see that there is more than one way to skin a cat and that being a sales person did not mean I have to change into a hideous freak show who spoke in a high pitched voice and wore pencil skirts and tottered around in stupid shoes that really made them look like they had carrots rammed up their bums. No it meant that I could be myself and I could do my thing in my way just as well as these strange shiny creatures from the textile world. (Note – I'm still working on my judgment skills)

Ask Yourself:

What do you have an inherent dislike for and why?

....

....

Have you ever taken yourself outside of your comfort zone just to see if you'd survive?

....

Do you like people judging you based on how you look?

....

....

....

....

Review of life to date

I had gone from the carefree backpacker with the world like the uncracked spine of a book to a woman in the cusp of marriage and settled down with two dogs. The past 10 years were fun, adventurous, crazy, drunken, hilarious, scary, overwhelming but most of all they shaped me. I am better for all of my experiences during this time. This is when I became Angie, it's when I decided what I wanted in life and how I was going to get it. My twenties gave me experience in work, life and love. I'd give my twenties a 10/10 if I were ever required to score my time on this planet.

IME MOMENT:
To start my own business - Garnish at age 30

After a little while a started to feel that funny feeling of discontent with the slowly declining world of commercial furniture and went to look for another opportunity. I came across a job as a Marketing Director (which made me laugh as essentially, I'd be directing myself) for a very small Freight Forwarding Company. I applied and got the job and the position title - haha.

In hindsight I think that no one else wanted the job because the boss was a little like a Tyrannosaurus Rex that hadn't been fed for over a year...

Anyway... my time learning about how freight worked and managing the sales and business development for this company highlighted one major fact – Queensland was the land of the small business and whilst everyone seemed to have an idea of how to run their businesses, not many of them were very good at marketing their businesses.

You may remember that with Kev's help I had started a small craft business when in Sydney, this was the start of "Garnish". I didn't really think that the whole craft thing had much legs and so I had let it go, so I started to toy with the idea of setting up a sampling business to consult into textile companies, but there were only a small handful of companies and the likelihood of them contracting the work to me was slim. Having worked with marketing departments for my entire working life made me aware of just what could and should be done to help these small businesses to improve how they were perceived and the messages they needed to convey. So with Kev's ever persistent encouragement, I decided to start a marketing company instead, no I haven't got a degree in Marketing and to be honest those people who do spend 3 years digesting text books in Uni still have no fucking idea about practical marketing anyway, so I was ahead of the eight ball there.

My first client was a friend of one of the ladies I account managed with the freight forwarding job, she and I had been to Fiji on a work trip and whilst in the expats hotel sipping on G & T's we discussed this new venture of mine and she was the first person to refer me into a company. And so with the support and encouragement from my hubby - Garnish Marketing was born. Jane still uses Garnish to this day 12 years on.

I decided to join a networking group called Leads Club, it was to be the kick start the business needed and illustrated to me just how much this type of business was required in the land of the small business. Initially I was terrified of going to this group. Remember that I was that person who "hated" sales people and would gladly stick pins in the ends of my fingers over talking to people I didn't know in a group situation just to "get to know them", but it bloody worked and my little marketing business started to generate interest, so I swallowed my pride and pulled up my big girl britches and got on with it. Now I enjoy networking (my younger self just swallowed some vomit).

I was literally running on faith and had no real clue of what I was doing, why or how I'd make this work, but I just kept going and networked my tail off. If I had not had the support from Kev this business would never have worked. He worked to earn the real money and I'd fanny about trying to get new clients for a few years initially. I learnt a lot in those first few years, I did a lot of work for free and I got ripped off a lot too, but 12 years later I'm still going and doing better than ever and have even found my niche within the manufacturing and engineering industries. Now I have a respected reputation in the industry and am seen as the go to for my chosen industry sector.

I carved the niche in those industries because quite simply, men are much simpler than females, they say when they can't do something like marketing and they ask for help and are happy to throw money at you to "just get it done".

Note: I have always found it remarkably easier to communicate with the male of the species anyway.

LESSON:
When you see an opportunity you take it, you jump in and take the bull by the horns and you do it. If you don't like what you are doing – then stop it. Get your ideas onto paper, talk to people, network and get on with it. Every single thing you do makes a difference. This is your journey so create your own path and don't sit back and wish you had, just do it. If you have to change a little bit about whom you are in order to get the most out of the new situation – just do it, see if it fits and then wear it with pride.

One thing about me, when it feels wrong, it's wrong, if it doesn't fit - it's time to move on. I've always loved my ability to just know, call it intuition, call it common sense (or uncommon sense), call it what you like, if you've got it – just use it.

Ask Yourself:

Have you ever had a huge idea that you really wanted to start working on but something stopped you?

Do you think you have the right tools to start working on your project? If not what are you missing?

IME MOMENT:
To marry Kev age 30

Everything was in place, our casual affair at a beautiful historic pub in Cleveland called The Grand View was all set up and ready to rock. Our wedding day was awesome; I'm no bridezilla, in fact if something had gone wrong, I'm not sure it would have actually mattered, I certainly wouldn't have cared. I knew that I had the right people in the right place, the stuff to get the wedding underway (you know dress, rings, catering, photographer, husband).

The ceremony was good, our dog Harvey was our ring bearer, he was so cute, I put some handmade turquoise cuffs on him and a turquoise collar and the rings were in a small silver chiffon bag around his neck. He was supposed to walk down the aisle nice and calmly and managed to do it perfectly in the rehearsal, but being a Chocolate Labrador when the time came to do it for real, he decided at the last minute to go in hunt of "that amazing smell". He didn't get far and it made us all laugh and managed to curb my nerves (which I had had for a few days prior).

My Mum and Dad came over from the UK and so did Kev's Aunt Clare, Uncle Phil and his young cousin Gracie too, which was amazing because I really miss my Mum and Dad and wish I could see them more often and Kev's Aunt, Uncle and cousin are lovely so it was great to have them as part of our big day. Kev's Australian based family came and all of our friends from Sydney came to Queensland to celebrate with us. It's the best party we have ever thrown; we haven't been able to top it yet – 13 years on. We forged some good memories that day...

We did the whole vow thing, got choked up, kissed, smiled and signed the contract to say that we would stick together through thick and thin. This has been referred to during the subsequent years – believe me.

We decided not to do the whole stuffy sit down dinner thing, so we cranked up the DJ, served cocktail style food and got on with what we do best – party and laugh our heads off.

We danced to 'Mr Bojangles' as our first dance, Robbie Williams did a cover of it a few years before and it had been our anthem since. Then as the night wore on, we started the dance offs and then 'I've had the time of my life' from Dirty Dancing came on and Kev and I did the lift. We still laugh about this to this day. My wedding dress sits in the back of my wardrobe in its protective cover with all of the dirt from the grass and the floor from that day. I don't want to wash away those happy memories, so dirty it will remain. Kev and his mates did some dodgy schoolboy renditions of break dancing (namely the worm) and we all laughed so hard.

I'd been in long-term relationships before but this one was different, Kev was different. Not only did I marry my best mate, I also married the class clown. There is not a day that goes by when he doesn't try to make me laugh. Be that by jiggling his bits whilst nude, singing daft songs, talking to me in silly foreign accents or just calling me to tell me about stupid stuff he has seen throughout his day. It's like being married to a child. It's a good relationship though. Naturally there are times when I'd like to smack him, or stab him in the forehead or maybe the eyeballs (the knife would glide better), or perhaps poison him with potassium chloride and bury his body in the garden, but they are few and far between - hmmm.

LESSON:
Let yourself feel. Remember the times that you felt full and complete. This will help feed you in the times when you'd prefer to stab that person in one of their orifices.

Ask yourself:

Do you remember a time when you felt content?

....
....
....

What do you think content feels like to you?

....
....
....
....

Do you think that what you consider as your "content" feeling will make you ultimately happy?

....

....

IME MOMENT:
To buy our first home in Clontarf and feel like I had grown up age 31

It's funny how buying a house and engaging in heavy debt means you've grown up, but that's what it felt like. We wanted to live on the north side of Brisbane. We lived on the Southside but the beauty and the seaside nature of Redcliffe really appealed to us, so we went house hunting.

We found this cute cottage style house that had only ever been owned by one family, it was perfect. The old man and his wife had raised a family of three girls there, they had flown the nest and started families of their own and so they felt it was time to move to a retirement village and enjoy their twilight years without the need to maintain a property and pool. I think the old man had literally fixed everything that was broken with number 8 wire. So much wire, we found it everywhere…

We put in an offer, they accepted and we bought our first house.
We loved living in this small house; it was a great starter home. So nice to have a pool too, coming from London, I felt rich!

It was in this home that we made lots of new friends, Garnish Marketing grew, we did our first renovation together which was surprisingly not that hard and I fell pregnant with our first baby – Jake.

Our Clontarf home was 900m from the water, so once Jake arrived, I spent a lot of time walking him down to the water to feed the pelicans and play at the park in between trying to run a business. Those days are a haze, we did so much and it felt like we achieved very little, but looking back I know that these days were just what we needed to be where we are today.

As time ticked on so too did the accumulation of "stuff" and it wouldn't be long before we outgrew this cottage dwelling for the dizzy bubble of North Lakes.

LESSON:
Life is a journey and every part has its role to play. Number 8 wire is incredible stuff.

Ask Yourself:

Do you remember the day when it felt like you had grown up?

....

....

....

....

....

IME MOMENT:
To fall pregnant with Jake (George inside name) and love growing another human being. Felt very special during pregnancy. Wrote a pregnancy diary Age 32

I would never describe myself as the maternal type. I don't go gooey over babies and I don't talk in high-pitched voices at the sight of small humans. So when I fell pregnant, after a year of trying and then assuming we couldn't have kids, I was amazed that I felt so very protective and special of my new little bump. I had my own Mexican jumping bean on board and I loved it.

I had been trying to fall pregnant for a year, we had been to doctors and naturopaths, taken horrible concoctions prescribed by naturopaths and done all sorts of things including 3am baby making sessions. (Someone told Kev that this worked, I seriously think that was just codswallop and some bloke wrote it in a magazine somewhere to make all the blokes happy so they had a legitimate reason to wake their partner up in the middle of the sodding night to "get some").

We were just coming to terms with the fact that maybe we weren't able to have kids and had chatted about the fact that if we couldn't maybe we could work and travel and love our dogs and do other things with our lives. We relaxed a bit and started to feel more positive so we took ourselves skiing in NZ, then when returned, I started to feel a bit dodgy and found out that I was in the early stages (3 weeks) of pregnancy. Amazing what happens when you relax eh!

The feeling of growing a baby is amazing, knowing that you are the home of a little person and that he or she eats, breathes and sleeps what you do is quite scary. Now remember that at this time I was pretty much single handedly running a marketing company with the help of a few select contractors to help. So 2 years into a new business and pregnant was a tad daunting. We had planned to have a baby though and the whole reason behind starting my own business (apart from the fact that employers were annoying) was so that I could still work whilst being a Mum. I did not relish the idea of being dictated to when trying to raise our first-born. (by now you'll realise I'm not that patient).

So maintaining a fully functional business with 12 businesses on my books was a tough gig with a newborn, but I muddled through and came out the other side, mostly unscathed. (I'm sure the slight twitch will subside one day). I have a distinct memory of having my palm pilot (smart phones were not about then) in the hospital bed checking emails literally a few hours after giving birth. Call it sad, call it what you like, but it was what happened. Jake had come 6 weeks early and I wasn't prepared for that. He had to stay in hospital for 6 days in the intensive care nursery, as he had not learnt how to suckle, as his suck reflex had not developed yet. So whilst he learnt how to feed I wrapped up some projects and got my contractors sorted with tasks for the first few weeks of Jake's life on the outside.

My milk hadn't come in either and so both Jake and I were not prepared for each other. We ended up having to do some bottle and some breast-feeding. It worked out well though to be honest as he drank milk like that blue Anteater on the Pink Panther sucking up ants. It hasn't hurt him; he grew faster than lightening and was off the chart in no time.

My whole family was in the UK and completely missed me being pregnant, so to try and include them I would send them emails with my pregnancy diary, a sarcastic tirade of experiences of a first time pregnant Pomme. I called it "The Diary of a Pregnant Pomme". My whole family would wait for the next instalment. My Mum actually made the emails into a book for me after Jake was born, I still treasure it. I've always toyed with the idea of publishing it one day...

But overall being pregnant was nice; it was an amazing feeling with thankfully very few vomit ridden days, maybe a bit of reflux but nothing too crazy. Kev made me feel very special during those months. I do remember Jake shoving his toes in between my ribs and swinging from my rib cage like some sort of monkey, which was painful. Then when I was closer to the end I was absolutely enormous. I had polyhydramnios, which meant that I was carrying far too much amniotic fluid in the sack and I was at risk of gestational diabetes. But other than that, it was good.

LESSON:
Life happens, relax and things will take their natural course. If you have made a commitment to do something do not let the fact that you have a

child stop you. Lots of people have children, it does not mean that your career has to end, it just means you need to be ultra-organised and be able to juggle being a mum first and a business person second.

Ask Yourself:

Are you at the stage in your life where you might like to have a child but you think you'd be compromising your career? Maybe re think your situation.

Is something in your life is not working out for you right now? If you took a step back and relaxed, maybe even forgot about it for a while you might just find it happens when you chill the fuck out.

IME MOMENT:
The Unexpected early arrival of George...

We had planned one last big day out six weeks prior to the expected due date of our first bub. We had a next-door neighbour whose little boy Josh was turning 1 on that day, so we were heading to his birthday party. Then we had booked tickets to see a theatre show in Brisbane (a matinee so I didn't fall asleep during the performance) followed by dinner with our good friends Nick & Jo in Ashgrove – we were going for Indian food. It was all set.

I woke early as usual with the need to pee, nothing unusual there; it appears that I had turned into a sieve.
Note – my bladder has never really recovered; I'm still a sieve.

Off I trundle to the loo, then something odd happened. My wee did not stop, it kept on going and going and going. I called Kev and he ran down the hallway.

"I think my waters have broken" I said.
"What no – it's too early" he said
"Yeah I know – but George doesn't"

So after a quick call to the Amity Team at the Redcliffe Anti Natal department off we hurtle to Redcliffe Hospital. It's strange being admitted to hospital to squeeze a child out when you're not mentally prepared for it. I had packed my bag just days before thinking it'd sit there and gather dust for a while, but no, no that wasn't to be.

The nurse came in, she had a quick look and said to me, in her Irish accent "well it looks like you're going to be having a baby today then Angie" and even though my waters had broken I was kind of shocked and replied "really". I'm not quite sure what I expected them to do – pop some gaffa tape over it and send me home and hope for the best??

My mate Bianca (whose 1 year olds birthday party we were supposed to be attending that very morning) had told me a few weeks before about how women in Africa have their babies and then go back to the field and work, we both discussed this and agreed that these women were hardcore. Bear this in mind shortly.

So I'm in the throes of natural labour, I had said only gas – no epidural even if I scream at you for it, so I was going through the motions of contractions, which were horrible. The fear started to kick in and I consciously held back from pushing even though these lovely ladies were doing their best in their soothing Irish tones to coerce me to "push honey' and that "I could do it' – well it turns out that I fucking couldn't and it hurt like all hell. I held back more and more and as time wore on we all got bored of this stupid game and I took a mental exit and zoned out, during this time they had me stand up to try and let gravity do it's thing, yep great idea as long as I don't need to tear myself a new orifice - whatever. During this mental escape I reminded myself about those women in Africa who just went back to work after popping out a baby, and so I grew a set of balls.

Without telling a soul at the next contraction I pushed with all my heart and soul and George came flying out like a rocket and bounced onto the mattress that I was standing over and snapped his umbilical cord. Everyone was surprised and no one was ready. Jake (now named) was lying on the hospital floor, there was blood everywhere and I was utterly exhausted. He was fine – they whisked him away to get his cord clamped. I got a few minutes of cuddles skin to skin, Kev got nothing and he was taken for 6 days into the special care nursery to grow a little more under the lights and work off his shock and jaundice.

It took 3 days for Kev to have his first cuddle of his first-born bubba. To this day – that story of the bungee jumping baby still circulates the halls of Redcliffe Hospital.

So that's how Jake came to planet earth and that's what happens when I commit to making a conscious decision. All hell breaks loose and shit flies everywhere...

LESSON:

It might be good to tell someone about monumental decisions you are about to make – otherwise everyone is shocked when it happens so fast with no warning.

I am capable of anything, if I set my mind to it, I can literally do anything. I am woman – hear me roar!!!

Ask Yourself:

Have you ever held back on doing something because of fear?

....
....
....
....

Have you ever shocked anyone by doing something they weren't prepared for – it might have been better to warn at least one person.

....
....
....
....

If you need to make a big decision, just do it, holding on to it makes the pain last longer.

IME MOMENT:
The art of delegation in small business. Age 33

As Jake started to grow, so too did the business. I'm one of those people who have an inherent fear of judgment and so letting clients down does not work for me. We started to get busier and busier at work and I could not handle it all with a small human in tow and so I started to take on some account-managing contractors to help me with the project management side of the business. Once I got this into place and everyone was trained it worked really well.

I'd always had graphic design and web designers as contractors but never had I had someone to help me with the client side of things. It was like being able to breathe again. I soon realised the benefit of delegating and outsourcing tasks and Garnish took on a whole new look and we've never looked back. That person I took on has been my right-hand woman for nearly 9 years, Vicky is incredible – we met at the ante natal clinic so we were both in the same boat, which means we get each other and really we just support each other.

Since these early days Garnish has always maintained a healthy portfolio of long-time loyal contractors who work for us. They work for other companies too, but they do a lot of work for Garnish and look after our clients like their own. It works really well for everyone involved.
The art of trusting someone else with a huge aspect of your business is hard at first but once you have broken free of those ties it is liberating and frees you up to grow the business and explore new opportunities.

LESSON:
This taught me that doing everything yourself is not necessary. It taught me that the art of delegation is imperative in business. It taught me how to trust other people whilst managing them. It taught me how to grow a business without going crazy and managing a new small family at the same time.

Ask Yourself:

Do you feel like you are only in control when you are doing all of the tasks yourself?

....

....

When was the last time you delegated a task to someone else?

....

....

IME MOMENT:
Fell pregnant with Zak (Alice was the inside name) again loved being pregnant but it was harder with a young son in tow this time. Age 33

Jake was 10 months old when I went to the chemist that day. I'd been feeling a little off for a week or so and it was a familiar feeling. Deep down I knew I was pregnant again, but I still felt the need to do at least 4 pregnancy tests. I should have bought shares in both Clear Blue and Rennie prior to having kids; the amount of money I've spent on these products is phenomenal.

So with a growing business, a fast-growing son and a busy hubby who was working hard and who had also started to coach the young Rugby League intakes at the Redcliffe Dolphins - life was hectic. However regardless of the frantic life we led, we were elated at the news that Jake would have a brother or sister soon.

We decided not to find out what sex the baby would be, however we did think that I might be carrying a little girl, so we gave the baby the inside name "Alice".

I have memories of taking the dogs for a walk/drag with Jake in his pram, me heavily pregnant and on the phone to clients absolutely exhausted. I also remember our good friend John chasing after my unruly Labrador 'Harvey' who felt the need to hump every passing dog even if they were on the other side of the huge park because I literally couldn't run. Kev was either at work or training a local football team and so this task was mostly left to me because otherwise we'd be trying to locate a brown coloured dog in the dark...

By this time, I had morphed into a phase of life I like to call "Mumsy" I was exhausted, chubby, stressed out and I had no time or inclination to look after how I looked or felt, all I did was feed, clean, work and walk the dogs. It was starting to drive me mad.

I have always struggled with making and retaining friends and so instead of doing something about it I carried on regardless and the seed of resentment sprouted some new leaves. I felt like Kev was always out, either at work (admittedly earning the majority of the cash that the family had) or training other people's kids to play football. Sometimes I was fine with it all and sometimes I got really fucking annoyed with it all. One thing I should note here is that through all my little moments of annoyance with Kev, he continued to 100% support me with my business that never really made a heap of cash and whilst we did have heated discussions about this at times, he never suggested that I go get a job. Kev has always been a great Dad and so this was never ever in question, I just sometimes felt alone.

Jake went to a family day care place two days a week so I had some time during the days to meet with clients and do some work, but it was hard work, however those days when I could get out and talk to adults were little breaths of sanity though and without them, I'm not sure if I would have made it through. Jake would sleep through which I am grateful about, but my body didn't let me sleep through with at least one wake up to answer the call of nature at night and to consume some Rennies to manage the acid reflux I seemed to be suffering from a tad more during this pregnancy.

Somehow it all worked out, most things do. Some days I was so tired I just gave in and was Mummy. I'd drag my ugly green shorts on and baggy beige vest and just give in. Some days I was so focused I got three days worth of work done in one hit. I'd work at night a lot, which was hard for Kev as I would essentially have to ignore him, but so much easier when you didn't have a small human to take care of. Those days I was more resilient than I've ever had to be, you get on with it and take the good with the bad.

Our house was becoming too small for our growing family, we started to consider doing an extension, but it would have completely over capitalised on the property and we would never have recouped the cost of the build and so we started to look for a new home that could house our family, dogs, cat and my growing business.

Although I was exhausted, I did have everything under control. I look back on these days and just say "wow" because it was hard work.

LESSON:
You cannot be superwoman all of the time. Growing a baby whilst looking after a baby and a business is hard work so give yourself a break. Be ready to juggle your day around to suit the needs of the family and clients. Its ok to say you are struggling or that you need your partner to help.

Ask Yourself:

Do you think that you are expected to be a superhuman all of the time?

When was the last time you took some time off?

....

....

....

IME MOMENT:
Moved to North Lakes 2 days after giving birth to Zak. Age 34

We found a 4-bedroom home with an awesome pool with a slide, it had space at the front for two offices, and it was big enough to house our growing collection of 'stuff' (not something I ever thought I'd have) but it was perfect. Before we bought in North Lakes we were told that we were entering "the North Lakes Bubble", I pooh poohed it off but it was like a vortex that sucked you in and you hardly ever came out. Everything you needed to survive was in this 3km circle. Some days it was great and some days it was stifling.

Bub was meant to have been born two weeks prior to moving day, but after the first overdue week the antenatal nurses decided that if he/she hadn't come naturally I'd be induced on the 16th December – two days before our set moving day. Great!

The little bugger was stubborn and decided to stay put, now this was harder work than you can imagine. By now you'll have realised that I live inside my head. I had been warned by the same Irish antenatal nurses that as I had Jake 6 weeks early, to "expect this baby to come early too".

The 16th arrived and Alice was still relaxing in the amniotic fluid with his/her feet resting on my rib cage (like his brother did) and was 2 weeks overdue, so in my head this bub was 8 weeks overdue – that's 2 months. It was time and I was over it and I just wanted it out of me. Then as we arrived in the hospital doors to be induced the contractions started naturally. Little Pest.

This meant that one-day before moving day Kev was in hospital with me while Alice entered the world and I would not be able to help at all with the move. (Nice one!)

Alice emerged fairly quickly as the slippery dip had been well oiled from Jake just 18 months prior and I was an old hand at this birthing lark now. As Alice made her way into the land of the Hammonds – she metamorphosed into Zak, Alice was a boy and a big one at that, he was huge, nearly 10lb and good god did I feel every oz. of him!

There was nothing I could do about not being there for the moving day apart from just let it happen, so after much persuasion from Kev, I did. Everything got done and I did not need to control a thing, it was actually quite refreshing and made me realise that Kev is really quite capable.

When I entered the hospital, I left our little Clontarf house for the last time and when we left the hospital stepped over the threshold of our new house in the North Lakes Bubble. It would be home for the next 4 years, and it was a great place to raise 2 small rambunctious boys.

We had a large home across the road from a decent sized lake which we could walk around and I'd eventually start running around to re gain my shape and take back some of the identity that I felt I had lost in the kafuffle of the last 5 years.

We made friends in North Lakes and like I was warned, there wasn't much of a need to leave the area very often. Occasionally I would escape just to prove that there was a universe outside of the 3km estate we lived in.

LESSON:
Let go of what you cannot control and go with the flow. Allow others to step in and help because one way or another everything will work out. Never lose your identity and if you do – get it back – quick smart.

Ask Yourself:

Are you a control freak?

Do you feel the need to micro manage everything?

What could you get the perfectly capable human at your side do to shrink your to do list?

IME MOMENT:
Grew the business even further when the Brisbane floods hit by reaching out to Roma. Age 35

Times were getting harder with the business; the GFC had hit and had taken a chunk of work away from us. Then the floods came to Brisbane and the customers we had left recoiled like the water before a tsunami hits. I had to diversify and look elsewhere for work if we were to survive this without me having to go find a job, which I hated the idea of. Can you imagine me going back into the workforce? I cringe at the idea of it.

At the time there was a lot of noise and opportunity in the West of Queensland where the APLNG pipeline was being laid. So instead of giving up and getting a job (remember my aversion to employers) I decided to see if I could get in on this and make my business grow. With Kev's support of me possibly spending time away from home from our very young family I put myself out there and made some connections.

I contacted the Maranoa Regional Council and asked the economic development office to help me to set up a series of roadshows across the council jurisdiction. They did and I ran one very successful marketing seminar in Roma and stayed in town for 3 days afterwards. Amazingly this gave me another 10 new clients and we were back in business and bigger than ever. I repeated the same thing in Dalby & Miles / Chinchilla again with success.

This meant that we started working with more industrial and rural types of businesses, which has literally shaped the type of Marketing Company we are today.

I like working out West; I like the Australian Bush and the real characters that live there. It's a no bullshit kind of world, which I appreciate immensely. That likely derives from my Dad who is also a no nonsense kind of man and makes himself clear with more expletives than is required most of the time. Anyway, it's like water off a ducks back to me and so I thrive out there.

I'm so glad I decided to take my business into this rural niche, I like the long drives and the expanse of the scenery. I like the smell of the eucalyptus and the heat of the sun beating down. I love seeing those rusty old windmills and half falling down timber sheds against the bright blue sky, it tells me that I'm far from home and on an adventure. Again this plays up my escapism in nature need. So not only does it bring me in better more solid loyal customers, it also feeds my need to travel, to explore and to go someplace new.

It also meant that I didn't need to feel like I wasn't contributing to the family, this is important to me as a strong independent woman.

LESSON:
If you come up against obstacles jump over then, don't let them stop you in your tracks. Diversify, seek other opportunities and believe that it will all work out – because one way or another, it will. Remember the story of my first business as a child, diversification helped me then and sure as hell helped me this time too.

Ask Yourself:

Have you ever had a huge obstacle stand in your way that threatened your livelihood?

....

....

....

Have you ever thought of diversifying what you do to get a better outcome?

....

....

....

....

There's got to be more...

IME MOMENT:
Had my first spiritual experience due to stress and feeling overwhelmed. Became 110% sure in life after death and other realms. Age 36

By now you've maybe come to the conclusion that this life I lead is jam packed - well you're not wrong. If we have ever had any tiny bit of space in the day, we throw in another something to do. If I'm honest it was too much, and every so often I melt down because of it.

At age 36, life became more full on than I could ever have imagined. With a now bigger set of clients to manage, 4 full time staff plus 3 contractors and myself, two young children, two dogs and a husband who worked and hated what he was doing and also coached a local rugby league team in the evenings, I started to feel the weight of the world on my shoulders and cracks started to appear in my armour, I was fucking knackered and really bloody over it...

There would be days where I would not get anything done, it felt like I was just chasing my tail doing the same thing again and again but with your team expecting you to have your shit together at 9am every day regardless because they appeared at the front door to start their day of work. In those days the team all worked from the two offices at the front of my house. So work invaded my home and I could not escape. It's a big part of the reason why we don't have staff working from my home office now.

I'm not sure if anyone ever realised how big my cracks were, but to me it was monumental. I was not coping at all, not one bit. The kids did go to day care for some of the time (as expensive as that was) I needed to compartmentalise sections of my day so I was not trying to be mummy, boss, wife all at the same time.

I started to get grumpy and moody and couldn't control it. Again, whether anyone realised this was happening was debatable because even though I had friends, I didn't really open up to many people and so it was my internal battle and I was trying to hide it. I had lost my identity and no longer felt like the Angie I have described earlier in this book; it was killing me.

That Mumsy character had taken over, I felt fat, ugly, tired, stressed out, unappreciated and downright fucking over it. I felt like I was doing everything; that all the childcare, house cleaning, food making and everything that we could have shared - was my job. (I know Kev did do some of it and looking back I think I was just in such a bad place that I exaggerated this in my head – I do that).

Then one day I burst. I decided that I needed to do something about this, so I cancelled work for the day and gave everyone the day off, I got the kids off to their day care place, Kev went to work and I decided that I'd either do something about this or at some point I'd do something stupid, which would not have been an option, but its how I felt at the time. That Black Dog still rears it's ugly head from time to time.

So I did 2 things so I had both professional and spiritual perspectives covered and I'd see what resonated with me the most. Note that I did not disclose to my husband that I felt like this and did not tell him that I was doing this. This was my journey and I needed to fix it myself. My biggest mistake...

- I decided to get some professional counselling advice; I booked a telephone consult with a lady that I had heard of through my work channels.
- I also decided to go and get a physical therapy session done like a massage or a healing too, but I had no idea what to ask for or what to expect.

NLP counselling did not work for me, I didn't respond well to the open-ended question format and it just made me want to hang up and scream.

The Natural Therapy place I knew was local and so I walked over. The lady who owned the place had said that they usually book out weeks in advance but today she had a cancelation at 11am and I could have that spot if I wanted. So I wandered back over at 11am not knowing what I was going there for. She asked me what I wanted and I said that I don't know but my energy is at an all time low and I'm always in a bad mood and I just want to not feel like this. She invited me into the room and I asked her what she would be doing and she said Reiki and Energy Healing work. I had no idea what Reiki was but I just trusted that it'd be good and lay down ready to experience whatever it would be – and that something literally changed my life.

I lay on the massage table in the dark room lit by musky smelling candles; prayer flags and nice quotes on banners adorned the walls. It was peaceful. Then Deb started to move her hands over my body without actually touching me. Never before had I felt the incredible tingling sensation that happened in that room on that day. Oddly enough, I felt that I had my Nan and Grandad (who passed away many years before and whom I hadn't thought about for years) in the room with me. In fact, it felt like someone was holding my hand and then placing their hand on my head. I just let Deb (the practitioner) do her thing and asked questions later.

It was like I was opened up on that day, I walked out of the room and all the way home feeling like I was walking on air, I was so ridiculously happy that I smiled and cried and talked to myself all the way home. I find it incredible that one simple energy healing can make such a profound difference to a person. I felt renewed and fixed. I wanted more.

I did ask what it was that I felt in the room and to my surprise she said it was an older lady with the initial M and her partner a male with the initial W. My Nan's name was Mavis and my Grandad was William even though everyone called him Bill. I had felt them; I was amazed and captivated with my first real psychic experience. I was hooked. I knew that I would need to find out more about this and how to do it again. That day illustrated to me that there is another realm; a place where our souls go and the veil between the worlds can be travelled between. It opened up a part of me that has helped me learn how to heal myself and ask for guidance from my higher self and my tribe of guides.

LESSON:
If you are not feeling right, do something about it; do not let life eat away at you. Regardless of how weird or unbelievable it is, try new things and be open to receiving something you might not expect.

Ask Yourself:

Have you ever had a time in your life where you felt lost, hopeless and just sad?

....
....
....
....

Are you open to all types of results and experiences as a result of the choices you make?

....
....
....

Would you describe yourself as an open person? The more open you are to new experiences – the more you will get out of them.

IME MOMENT:
Decided to do a Reiki course, this was the catalyst for change in me and a deeper understanding of "life" - Age 36

After my initial foray into the energy-healing world I knew I wanted more. The only way to find out more was to learn and so I did a weekend course in Reiki 1 and 2. Little did I know that this would be the tip of the iceberg and would water the seed of curiosity in me that I didn't know existed.

The teachings were not all that interesting and none of the theory really stuck with me. But a simple exercise using clay did stick with me, the ability to send my own energy to parts of myself and others stuck with me and an overwhelming sense of a spirit's presence has stuck with me so much so that I can tell when I am close to a spirit or they are close to me. (Yeah that sounds odd I know, but it's so very true). I literally get a tingling sensation, which for me comes when whoever is close wants to confirm that what I am doing is right. I also get it as a warning when something is up ahead, so I'm more aware of those moments and look for the possible problem, or feel safe in the knowledge that what I'm saying is right.

Like I said - the clay exercise was good, it's something that I do with my kids today, they love it. Basically you take 22 small pieces of air drying clay and turn them into little flat stones. On each stone you write a letter and let them dry.

On 7 you write the letter G for Grateful
On 7 you write the letter D for Detach
On 7 you write the letter M for Manifest
On 1 you write the letter U for Unify

Each day you take a stone (or a wish as I call them with my kids) and you throw the stone into a body of water or plant it in the earth. The idea is that the clay needs to go back to the earth for the Universe to provide. It's a way of consciously choosing what you think about. It takes 21 days to change a habit – so it's perfect for rewiring your thinking and actually something really nice to do.

So randomly you select the stone and you either say
I am Grateful for XXX
I want to Detach XXX
I would like to Manifest XXX

Then on the 22nd day you take the Unify stone and you throw that one in last of all to bring the ceremony to a close.

It's therapeutic, it makes you think about what you want and what you want to detach, it also makes you realise that you have at least 7 things to be grateful for and that is such a good thing. Being grateful every day allows you to start the day in the most positive manner. To this day I have a jar at the side of my bed and regularly I write on a small piece of paper what I am grateful for on that day. Once a year I go back over those notes and see how lucky I am to be grateful for so much. It's a healing process in itself.

Here's a little story for you
Flowers in a bottle from Thailand Is all about how being grateful helps.

We went on a family holiday to Thailand and decided to go and do the Sea caves Kayak tour as it was something fun that the kids could do as well and it looked awesome. So off we went to the other side of Phuket Island to catch the boat. The guides were genuinely nice guys and did everything they could to make us feel comfortable. One of the guides took a shine to our family and we were his responsibility. Now I'm not silly enough to think that they were not playing up to us because we were tourists, but I felt genuinely looked after and like they gave a damn. Now to me that is the best kind of customer service and it's a trait that most westerners sadly lack.

After a hearty lunch at the end of the boat and kayak tour, which was great, we started to head back towards the harbour and land. The guides all got some small water bottles that had been used during the trip and some coloured straws out. They made each child on board a Fish and a Fishing rod out of these straws and for each lady on board they made a small water bottle filled with coloured straw flowers. They painstakingly made each one in front of us and presented them to us with a warm handshake. To me this was a gesture of gratitude beyond anything I have experienced before. To this day the bottle of straw flowers sits on my office desk reminding me to be grateful and that the power of gratitude is huge.

Another story about being grateful for what you have

Here is another excerpt from my China experience.
Duncan and I (the guy I was with at the time) had discussed having a truly authentic experience opposed to the sugar-coated version a lot of Westerners experience.

With that in mind we booked into a basic hotel in the back streets of a fairly ordinary part of town, that clearly wasn't meant for tourists – lets put it that way. The morning after the first night we went out in search of something to eat for breakfast and to be honest struggled to locate anything as it's all laid out so differently in China. So with a grumbling tummy we located a convenience store and found something we could munch on, there was a park around the corner so we decided to sit down and eat there. What we found astounded me. Bear in mind that we were in a very poor part of town where people were riding around on bicycles without tyres – so just on their metal rims. We witnessed a family of people living in what looked like a garden shed which had 2 beds in it – one for the grandparents, one for the parents and the children slept on the floor. They burnt their toilet paper in the metal drum in the street and brushed their teeth in the run off water in the gutter. I wish I could say I was making this up but the fact is, I'm not. So we were in this park having a bite to eat ready to take on the sights, smells and sounds of Beijing and all of a sudden people came from everywhere as piped music started to play. Couples joined hands and on a cracked concrete section of the park that was gated off with rickety old metal gates - they started to ballroom dance.

Dressed in their tattered clothing they gracefully took the floor and for that moment in time, they were free, liberated and happy. In the far corner of the park several groups of people doing Tai Chi gathered, working effortlessly in unison to free them from old age, to keep them limber and to connect them to their highest and best selves. It was a sight to behold and one that has stuck with me ever since.

What does this teach me?
Every time I feel disgruntled or stuck, or I'm frustrated because of something that has happened at work or at home I think of this moment and realise that I have so much and yet I am feeling like I'm hard done by, yet these people literally have nothing but the make the most out of the life they have and for those moments they are more free than I will ever be because their mindset is so beautifully aligned with their spirit instead of stuff, time and the dreaded to do list.

Be more like the graceful ballroom dancers or the people doing tai chi and realise that you are lucky, you are alive and this is to be celebrated.

I believe that it does not matter what you do for a job, what you achieve or what you fail to obtain, none of that matters. Everything on our Earth is an illusion. We are creating our own perception of our world and we respond to situations uniquely. What matters is that whatever we do, we do with grace, with a view to being the happiest most fulfilled person we can be. This is our soul's path, this is what we are here to learn and the location, time and environment we are placed into to fulfil this sole purpose is part of the test. Remember that Earth is a classroom and the lesson is your life.

LESSON:
If you yearn for more information, do something about it. You will learn more than you'll ever realise and you may even start to do things differently and see the world in a better way. Be grateful, show your gratitude and be humble.

Ask Yourself:

Do you find yourself always searching for the next big thing? Maybe it's in your heart, maybe that big thing is acceptance of what is.

When was the last time you thought about what you are grateful for?

When was the last time you decided to detach a part of you that no longer serves you?

If you had the chance to manifest something – what would it be?

How do you show that you are happy to be alive?

IME MOMENT:
Decided to move to The Sunshine Coast Age 37

Kev and I have been slowly creeping north since we met. First Sydney, then Birkdale (South of Brisbane), then Clontarf (North of Brisbane) North Lakes (even further North of Brisbane) and so it was pretty normal to take then next step and move up to The Sunshine Coast (even further North than that).

It had always been the place that we decided that we wanted to end up, so why wait for the perfect time, why isn't now the perfect time. It is and so here we are. We found ourselves up the coast at least once a month so Kev could surf and then we enrolled Jake in Nippers and it became a weekly thing. The Sunshine Coast is like a magnet to us both, pulling us in and making us love it. So why not live where you love, waiting for the perfect time is just daft, just do it.

We wanted the boys to grow up near the beach and so we bit the bullet and sold the big home and moved to Burnside, not quite where we want to end up, but close enough for us to experience life on the coast. The next stop will be a larger home with a pool. It's a five-year plan that we will have sooner, because that is just what we do – a friend of mine calls us "over achievers", I guess it's better than under achieving.

The year we moved Kev also decided to start his own Business. Not content with working for a Company that employed Australia's rudest manager, he too sought better things and has a bigger vision for his life. It's why we are connected; we are both driven and passionate.

So Kev started Garnish Projects & Maintenance, its 5 years in now and is going great guns. Kev has the ability to make things happen, a lot of the time he is a lot like a bull in a china shop, but I can be too. He knows what he wants and will not let anyone or anything stand in his way. It's why he is doing well. I'm proud of the way he manages the jobs and clients he has. He believes in doing a good job once and he believes in transparent communication. It's rare to find a tradesman who will communicate properly and so he is winning client after client from referrals for his efforts.

So now we are two gung-ho entrepreneurs who won't take no for an answer and strive to achieve. Slowly we will take over the Coast...
Moving to the Sunshine Coast also meant that Kev was able to let go of Footy and take up the sport of Triathlon. It wasn't an immediate transition,

he had a good 9-month break from doing anything at all, but he needed to do something. So when he decided upon triathlon he got right into it and really fit in a short period of time. It made me aware of my shortcomings and my inability to make friends and do new things. Instead of me being proud of him, I harboured seeds of jealousy. Yes, Yes I am really quite dumb – I know.

LESSON:
Dreams are there for you to turn into reality. Do not wait for the perfect time to grasp a hold of life and live it.

If you don't like something – fucking say something. Learn from my mistakes – please!

Ask Yourself:

Are you living where you want to live?

....

....

Are you doing the job you want to do?

....

....

Are you passionate about your life?

....

....

Are you waiting for something better to come along?

_____

_____

Are you waiting for the right time?

_____

_____

Here's a tip: Decide what you want (for now), it doesn't need to be a 10 year or forever goal, but have a goal, strive towards something or you'll just plod, you'll stagnate and you'll bore yourself to tears.

IME MOMENT:
Started attending Gnosis classes and started to meditate properly.
Age 37

Learning never stops with me. I like to read and learn new things. After the whole Reiki experience back in 2011 I yearned to learn more. I have devoured many books and have been to a number of meditation classes but I felt like I wanted information as well as practice.

Now religion has never been on my agenda (remember at the age of 11, I told my grandparents that church wasn't for me), but I have always been of the belief that there is more than this, there has to be more than this. There have been so many documented cases of the fact that there is more than this that I cannot simply ignore this and put it down to the fact that every individual had simply gone doo-lally.

I found a course on Gnosis, which aims to work on the workings of the inner self and how we can be harmonious in ourselves and in our surroundings without praying to a God as such.

The course showed me that we are more than just this collection of flesh and bones, that we have a number of bodies and although you cannot see them does not mean that they do not exist.

HERE'S A SHORT SYNOPSIS

We consist of:
- Our Dense Physical Body you can see, touch and feel.
- Our Vital Body – our fears and desires
- Our Astral Body – where we go when we dream
- Our Mental Body – Our opinions and thoughts
- Our Causal Body – exists in the karmic realm
- Our Buddic Body – this is our divine soul
- Our Atmic Body – our intimate body – where we find self-mastery

Imagine the other bodies as fields that surround your physical body. You hurt one of them, it will affect the others.
It taught me that we live in our projections & fantasies both in the past & in the future. Often we do not live in the consciousness of now. It's a mistake. All we have is now. We cannot change the past and dwelling on the 'what if' of the future is silly, because it might never come. So we must live in the present.

It taught me that time moves slower or faster for each individual depending on how fast or slow they vibrate at. Have you ever noticed how some people can get so much more done than others even though neither person is lazy? It's just that the person who gets so much done is vibrating on a higher frequency than the other. It's not right or wrong, it just is…

It taught me that we are not what we are based on what we have been through.

What we go through and what happens to us is based entirely on what we are internally.

It taught me that there is a reflection of yourself in everyone you meet. So if, you don't like something about someone, there is something about you in that respect that you also do not like. Remember that Earth is a classroom and we are here to learn specific lessons.
It taught me that we are on this planet to experience life not to hoard or self-destruct.

It taught me that there are 4 kingdoms:
- Mineral Kingdom
- Plant Kingdom
- Animal Kingdom
- Human Kingdom

At various stages of our many lives we evolve from the Mineral Kingdom through the Plant and Animal Kingdoms and into the Human Kingdom. Some people are not as far along the evolutionary path as you and so some people may act more like animals (some even more like rocks) than humans, but that is because in terms of being a human, they are young and have only had a few goes at it. Those humans that are wiser and have less ego attached to them have been around a few times more and have learnt some more of those important lessons. So, forgive those who appear to be dense, they are not as advanced as you. Give them time. Even if you do not believe this, you can see that this could be so true for some people on our planet who have clearly not evolved yet. This is not a judgment – it's my opinion. Think about it though.

It taught me that everything is energy and this took me back to my Reiki teachings where I was healed through the shifting of my energies. So not only do I understand that we are all energy I have felt the physical difference we can make by moving our energy around and dissolving bad energy. I now know that we can have bindings attached to us from past lives and so we must be energy because you cannot take this from body to body it has to be something we cannot see.

It taught me that the personality is based on memory.
We experience things and this leaves us with an impression.
Our senses allow our mind to compare, judge, react and remember those times.
Your impressions are the energetic thoughts we receive.
Whether they are pleasant or unpleasant they come through our senses
Our Mind stores our sensations and turns them into memories.
The accumulation of sensations produces perception or concepts, which leads to a development of language and behaviours.
This tells me that our experiences create our impressions and ultimately drives our behaviour and other people's perceptions of you.
This is what drives us forwards or blocks our way as developing humans.
We live in our own projections / fantasies from the past and of the future, few of us live in the consciousness of now.

It taught me about Belief systems and why it's not important what you believe, just that you believe in something. Having a catalyst helps to direct your focus, once you focus you become empowered, once you are empowered your actions are more powerful and when you act using your internally focused and empowered influence your results are unimaginable. I don't care if you believe in a god, a source, a universe, your family, yourself, your chosen sporting team, your dog – it doesn't matter.

So, as a teaching from this Gnosis course it allowed me to understand that I am not just what I see in the mirror, I am my behaviour, my impressions, my experiences, my belief system and all of these things affect my many bodies in this realm and the others. It has opened my eyes to the fact that this is not "it", that we have so very far to go both as individuals and as a collection of energies. We sculpt our own existence and the faster we accept the truths the sooner we move through the kingdoms and rise to become an energy that leaves a good impression on our universe.

Through meditation I have begun to feel more, to be able to connect with my other bodies and to assimilate all of the daily shenanigans that take place and not allow these sensations to become debilitating emotions so I do not develop ego filled responses to situations and that I am a nice person who is fulfilling her purpose.

When we learn to control our breath, we can control our minds and when we can quiet our minds we are free. Imagine...

LESSON:
Every action we take is like a blank cheque to the future so you are carving your own path and if you understand the principles of who we are, how we are and why we are you will enjoy your experiences ten-fold and become free.

Ask Yourself:

Do you have a belief of anything?

....

....

Think about the way that you run your life. Do you think that your energy and the way you run your life affects others energy and the way they run their lives?

....

....

....

Can you think of someone who you feel is less evolved than others?

....

....

IME MOMENT:
Realised what my purpose is – age 37

Amidst all of my challenges I do have moments of complete clarity – amazingly. But, I've figured it out; I worked out what my purpose is.

It is to help business people achieve their business dream but to keep them realistic and on track, small, medium and large businesses alike. So Garnish Marketing really is the catalyst for me to deliver this service and that too will evolve.

I have been put on this earth to help people realise their destiny and strive for their best, especially in a business sense. When I meet a new client or prospect, I thrive on the initial meeting; it's the part of my role that I enjoy the most and where I am absolutely my most genuine authentic self. I get so into what I am doing that ideas just fill my head. Sometimes it feels, as though it isn't me speaking, I am sometimes amazed at the words that come out of my mouth.

Maybe I am being spoken through - who knows, but my clients love it and they engage me to come back just to talk to them and inspire them every month. The time I spend with these people in the beginning helps to build trust, which I think is the building block to a successful long-term relationship. Connecting with each other as humans is vital, you cannot possibly deliver well thought out, and heart filled, targeted marketing campaigns without understanding WHY they are doing what they do. It's all about creating a conscious connection with your customers.

The core thing to take from this is that you will create your hearts desires by giving, not taking. Sure, I get paid for my role, but I get great satisfaction from what I do and quite often I over deliver and help people out that cannot afford to use me because I know that I am here to share my talent. I'm creating true value and building a reputation as someone who truly helps people realise their visions. Its why I mentor as a volunteer for a Government run program – its important to give back.

My dreams tell me that I'm here on this planet to help, to give back, to encourage and develop other peoples' ideas and dreams into well planned out realities. I pay attention to the messages I get in my dreams; quite often they are poignant and important, same for the messages I get when I meditate, the trick is to listen and watch, the more you open your eyes and ears the more you'll see the messages.

Its funny how many people I randomly meet that need to hear something and I know just what they need to hear, so I tell them and their day changes, their faces lighten and they feel better. It's a great gift and I like to share it, although I only use it when I feel compelled to. It's led me into more of a mentoring role now, which I really enjoy. So I'm letting the ball roll, nurturing its path to where I am most comfortable (industry and manufacturing) and accepting that when I meet people randomly that I more than likely have a reason for the new connection and I pay attention. It's making my business grow, it's growing me as a person and I'm enjoying my career progression as a result.

LESSON:
Listen, pay attention and be open to opportunity – for therein lies the very reason you are here.

Ask Yourself:

Have you figured out what your purpose is yet?

Do you pay attention to the things that happen day to day with you?

Have you noticed that you'll meet a certain type of person more often than others?

Do you sometimes say things and wonder where the hell that came from?

IME MOMENT:
Time to learn how to...

So at the age of 38/39 with my newfound clarity, I decided that it was time to start doing some of those things that I had been putting off. For years I've been making excuses as to why I cannot do the things that I want to do. No time, kids come first, got work/shit to do, hubby needs me to do XYZ.. blah blah blah, the list is endless and boring. After 6 years of not doing much that I wanted because I'd had kids and had somehow lost most of my identity in the process, I decided that perhaps maybe, just maybe I could reclaim a bit of myself. No time like the present and so I started to meditate, draw, paint, play with clay, race in triathlons and I started to learn how to surf plus I picked up the guitar again. I'd had it to the back teeth of feeling like I should come last. I constantly felt like I needed to escape and waged a constant war between the often-unobtainable balance between work, mum, wife and me.

Triathlon: Now first off let's just say that swimming has never been my forte and so starting to train and then compete in triathlons was a huge step for me. Participating in Triathlon was not my idea; it was my husband's thing. He could see what I couldn't see, that I would actually (at some point) enjoy doing this sport. Initially it was bloody hard work, I was 10kg heavier than I should be and felt pretty unfit.

Most triathlons have open water swims, so it's not like you are following the black line of the pool and can just jump out or stand up when you think you can't do it anymore. No, you are out in the water thrashing about with a hundred other plastic cap clad ladies who are all as competitive as a pit bull in the ring. I'm much better at it now and can even swim a 3km distance now. In September of 2014 I couldn't swim 200m without feeling like my heart might explode, so I'm pretty happy with this progression. I've recently completed my first half IronMan, so I'm pretty proud of that. The cycling and running I knew I'd be OK with as I've always been a runner and I've cycled everywhere (on a mountain bike mind you) purely because I've always been a skint student or traveller and didn't learn to drive until I was 27. I call myself a participation athlete though as the thought of trying to win one of these makes me shudder. If I get a good position at the end, I'm happy, if not I'm happy.

Saying that though – although I've never been a very competitive person, I must have a slightly competitive streak in me because when I'm in the race I pick a chick and hunt her down till I pass her now. I guess the reason I got into triathlons is because Kev my hubby started doing it and then so did our kids and I really didn't want to be one of those overweight mums that stand on the sidelines and just watch. I'd prefer to be part of it and have a crack than say "oh no I couldn't do that" Sod it – do it. I now see it as fun, I see the training as a lifestyle choice and the friends I've gained from it have improved my life. The whole triathlon community especially on the Sunshine Coast is so supportive. So I can proudly say "I do like the sport and the camaraderie".

Surfing: The surfing was another big step as again it meant facing a fear of the ocean. Now I'm an English woman and so my head goes into "there's a shark in there" territory as soon as I get into the ocean. As a child we rarely spent any time in a seaside location and if we did our time in the brown murky waters were short lived, shallow and we were being transported by dad in a rubber dinghy. (I have a memory of me and my sisters being swept out to sea in the dinghy and Dad having to swim out to save us – oops, sorry Dad). As an adult, I also believed that I was too big (80kgs at that time) and not coordinated enough to be able to stand up on a surfboard. Wrong and wrong again, I can do it and in fact most time I go to stand up these days I actually catch the wave, so I can do it, not well, but I'm doing it. I had a good surf teacher in Steve; he was patient and kind to me even when I was not being very brave. The other ladies were also all learning and it was fun instead of embarrassing. We combined yoga and surf, which was cool; it was a lovely thing to do in the mornings. I don't do surf lessons anymore and I miss my little group, I really must make time to catch up with them.

I felt a bit like "adventure mum". I started to surf because my young two boys surf and so does Kev my hubby (he's actually quite good at it) and so it's something I was missing out on. I needed to be able to get into the water with the boys in case something ever happened. Good job I did because there was a time when we were on holiday in Byron Bay on Mothers Day 2015 at Wategos Beach when the surf was a little wilder than I might have liked (Note:- I prefer small bumps – not actual waves).

We went into the surf and proceeded to paddle out the back to where it was calmer so we could pick our waves, but Zak stopped paddling (for some unknown reason) and got caught in a rip. I quickly realised and paddled hard and fast to try and get him back on track but it caught me too and we got swept towards the rocks. I managed to get him before he collided with the rocks and got rid of the board, which was making him travel too quickly into the rocks, and we clambered over the rocks. Two old surfer dudes saw what was happening and came to save us, taking our boards and carrying Zak to safety. It was frightening. I now will not surf at a beach with rocks – lesson learnt.

I think that event scarred both Zak and I for life. I was slightly petrified to get back into the water after this, I didn't actually realise how scared I was until I was back in the ocean and I started shaking. Kev encouraged us to get back into the water immediately so we didn't build up our own little barrier of fear for the future. It worked for Zak immediately. But later that day at another beach break, I had another accident of my own in the water. After getting the boys to go under a particularly heavy shore-breaking wave, I missed the timing and got picked up by the wave. It collected me and smashed me face first into the sand and broke my nose, I walked out of the water with blood all over me and a fucking huge head-ache. Shit day really. We went straight to the pub, I needed a drink. However, saying that I am over the fear of the ocean now and have more respect for it as a result. Now, I compete in ocean swims now have an ocean wetsuit for swimming in (it's really just a big buoyancy aid). It's important to note that you can get over a fear if you confront it – head on.

Guitar: When I was a child, I started to learn the guitar, but Mrs Ainsley my teacher, was very religious and had us playing sodding hymns, it was so boring so I put the guitar down. Good King Wenceslas – no thank you!

When I came to Australia I picked it up again and went to lessons in Sydney with Mr Foley who I think may have gone to the same school as Mrs Ainsley, far out these people were so incredibly boring. Yankee Doodle – really? for adults... Hmmm no thanks. So yet again I nicked off. So at the tender age of 38 I picked up the six stringer again and had a third crack at it. I'm now playing songs I like and am able to sing along with some of them. I'm enjoying it because its something I like that I can do. My favourite tunes to play include Wish you were here by Pink Floyd, Wonderful Tonight by Eric Clapton, a couple of easy Eagles tunes and some Van Morrison. Plus Kev bought me a beautiful Cort Guitar to play on – I love it, again it's something I need to keep plugging away at.

LESSON:
It's never too late to teach an old dog a new trick. If I can do it – you can too. You might make mistakes, some might hurt but you should not let it stop you.

Ask Yourself:

What is the one thing that you've always wanted to have a crack at?

....

....

What do you think is stopping you from starting to learn a new skill? Do you think that you are past it? / Do you think that you wouldn't be able to do it? Do you think that people would laugh at you? Unpack it.

IME MOMENT:
Attended a past life regression workshop in Melbourne – age 39

Clearly I'm still learning new skills and am keen to open new doorways. I had previously had a past life regression session years ago in Brisbane, but never really did anything with it after that.

I started on this spiritual path because I needed something to hang onto, I'd been in a depressive state for a while, I was continually overwhelmed with all of the commitments I had with the business, kids, husband and everything else I jammed into my life. Like a lot of middle aged people, you start to get overwhelmed and feel like the weight of the world is on your shoulders. I started to wonder why, what's the point and what is this all leading to.

I like the idea of learning lessons as you go (otherwise why go through all this crap if you are not actually getting something out of it).
I like the idea that there has to be mOre, there has to be a reason. I like the idea that we take a little of each life from existence to existence and that all of our lives matter. So, I started to explore that concept and came across past life regression.

No, I did not start wearing purple chiffon tops and velour long skirts and a headscarf.

At this time of my life, I started to read Dr. Brian Weiss's books all about past life regression, which blew my tiny mind. The thought that some of these people have experienced so much about themselves in past lives through a simple meditation makes my heart sing, so I was eager to learn more. Then I heard that Dr. Brian Weiss was coming to Australia to do a 2-day seminar/workshop in Melbourne. I spoke to Kev about it. True to form he did a bunch of research, looked into flights, accommodation and secured my ticket for the event. I was actually going, it was so exciting. My ticket was booked and off I went. It meant that I got a break from everyday life, I got to explore something I liked on my own and I got to catch up with my old mate Vic from my London days.

During this weekend through a group meditation I experienced a few things and discovered a couple of past lives that actually represent some of the fears I have in this life now as Angie.

I discovered that I was a Native American Indian Chief and that my now husband Kev was the General of the opposing army. He and his army killed my entire tribe except me. So I scalped him. I deduce from this that this may be where he might think I bite his head off at times.

I discovered that I was the lesbian lover of a royal Princess and that this was forbidden. I was dragged from my lovers' bed by none other than Kev who was leader of the Kings Guard and sentenced to death by arrow – he shot the fatal arrow right through my heart. This explains why I am not averse to the idea of being bi sexual and why when I let Kev down my heart literally aches.

So I have been a failed Chief who killed my now husband and a lesbian lover who has killed by my now husband. How bizarre. I guess we have spent some life times together in some way shape or form mutilating each other until this one when we are together as man and wife. The mutilation continues in this life just emotionally instead of physically (as you will see). I wonder what the next life will bring.

LESSON:

Its OK to explore past versions of yourself. It helps to identify the parts of this life that still need work. I guess the lesson I should be taking from this is that it is important to stand up to others in this life, I'm the boss of me and no one else. You do you and I'll do me.

Ask Yourself:

Have you ever wondered if you'd had past lives with someone close to you?

....

....

Have you ever wondered who you were in a past life?

....

....

Do you think that any of the emotions or impressions you learnt in a past life could ever somehow miraculously be present in this life in this for as you?

....

....

....

IME MOMENT:
Attended a weekend silent retreat at an Ashram

These years of my life were sometimes harder than they needed to be, and mostly because I thought about shit FAR TOO MUCH. At times I felt the distinct need to escape and Kev knew I had this inherent need to get away which meant that he'd either book or support my need to escape for a few days every six months or so. It was self-preservation from two sides of the coin – his and mine.
I wanted to do something that connected all the parts of me and so my surfing instructor Steve told me about this retreat weekend that he had been to years before, he said how much he got out of it. I told Kev about it, he looked into it (knowing I never would) and booked me in, so one weekend off I trundled into the Byron Hills. I wanted to go, not really sure why I don't acknowledge what I want and book in things for myself. (Self sabotage maybe?).

I'm glad Kev booked it and I'm glad I went. I felt like I was missing something. I'd gone back to being angry and feeling like I had too much on my plate again (it's so easy to slip back into old and bad behaviours). Steve thought that perhaps I needed to realise that I was enough and to go to a place like an Ashram was going to be a journey into loving myself and being authentic with strangers. He was right. Kev needed me to be me again; I needed to be me again so this was for us both.

However, initially I felt like a fraud, everyone else was so liberated and free in his or her hippie-ness (I do believe that most of it was ego though). There was one particular young girl who was about 18 and she liked to walk about topless and hug everyone then suddenly fall into a heap of tears and one other girl who was mid-twenties who literally cried non-stop – I felt like poking her eyes out just to give her something to cry about (how Neanderthal-like of me). Anyway, I guess they had their hearts **wide**-open, (vomit) silly moos. (Still working on that judgment)

It was a nice weekend though and weirdly enough it was a silent retreat, which was OK, as I didn't really want to say much anyway. We did lots of meditation and some strange stuff like laughing, hugging and shaking meditations, which oddly enough make you, feel very euphoric when you let go and just got into it.

After a few hours I just gave in to the "that's weird" sensation and just went with the flow and had an amazing time.

I still think about that weekend, the silent connections I made were intense and the space to be whoever you want to be was liberating. I should do it more often. I'll never see these people again and it was not a physical or even mental connection I made with any of them. If you asked me any of their names, I would have no clue but the spiritual connection was intense. It was just a meeting of energy and literally nothing more.

LESSON:
If it's weird, it's not necessarily wrong, it's just not what you've done before. Remember the lesson about your impressions ultimately carving out your behaviours. Sometimes it's fun to let go and embrace new things.

Ask Yourself:

Have you ever felt like a fraud?

....

Have you ever been in a room and felt like you didn't belong, but then ended up giving in, joining in and enjoying it?

....

....

....

Do you think that your impressions create your behaviours and that sometimes our first impressions need to be reviewed with your "heart wide open"?

....

....

....

IME MOMENT:
Premature Realisation – Age 39

At the grand old age of 39 – I had finally come to the conclusion that I was a good person, I was more grounded than I had been for a long time, and I felt that at the time I did whatever I could to help people in my life. At this stage of my life I can say that I felt that I loved my life and my family. I had a few really good mates who I owed a lot to. I felt like I had gotten through some of the harder parts of bringing up young kids and that I was alright. Look, marriage had its ups and downs, Kev and I fought about stupid shit a lot – we still do - but it appeared that everyone was in the same boat.

I'm the kind of chick who loves the outside and being in the forest. My goals at this stage were to simply be grateful for the opportunities that life gave to me, to detach my attachment to money or the lack of it (I have issues with spending money on myself that stems from a feeling of lack), and to walk confidently through the portal to my own true path of destiny. I felt like I was on the right path to fulfil my destiny, which is one that brings happiness and along the path manifests success. Now I'm starting to sound like one of those goddamn hippie's - right? Queue the rolling of eyeballs.

It's where I was at that time of my life. All of the lessons that I had experienced from birth to now and all of those conscious decisions equipped me with the tools I needed to forge ahead. I was confident that I had this; I was Angie Hammond - in control of my own destiny and living a life that is true to my purpose. (The bucket is full, use the sink to vomit more).

Then it all changed...

LESSON:
Enjoy the times when you realise that you're OK and that you have this shit down pat. You'll need those days when the brown stuff hits the fan.

In the moments that you feel so happy and secure hold those memories dear because it could just be the warning that all hell is about to break loose and fuck this shit up!

Ask Yourself:

Have you reached the conclusion that you are enough and completely adequate yet?

....

....

....

Do you realise just how amazing you are and what a great job you are doing?

....

....

....

IME MOMENT:
Awarded the Gumby Award!

It was November 2015, I was alright with who I was, sure of myself and confident in the fact that what I was doing was true, correct and I was on my "destiny path".

But Kev and I had been niggling at each other for a while now and I was starting to lose my shit more often than was normal. I was felt like I wasn't enough for him. He'd talk about the people at triathlon so often, and yeah I was involved (to a point) but someone still had to look after the boys when training was on. I'd always put my hand up for it because I knew he wanted to train and I didn't really give much of a shit about being the next elite athlete, but instead of me accepting my own damn decision I added it to my seed of resentment which was flourishing by now.

I felt like I was trying so damn hard to make my business work that it quite possibly overtook my world so from Kev's perspective, this probably gave him the shits too. So, we ended up rubbing each other up the wrong way. I'd talk about work, he'd talk about triathlon, and we didn't get each other's worlds. It's a recipe for disaster.

We both entered the local business awards that year and naturally (as I'm sure everyone else who entered did) we both got through to the finals (they have to sell tickets to their Gala event somehow, right?).

We'd been surfing that morning (remember I'm very uncoordinated) and I managed to cop the surfboard into my head after falling off of a very small but messy wave. Immediately a large bruise appears on my cheekbone. We all laugh, it's my fault, I'm not great at this sport (not for the want of trying mind).

Wearing more make up than a transvestite in Thailand, off we trot to the awards night. More than a few drinks later we end up arguing. It was unnecessary but an event that stuck in my mind. We both just wanted to have a good night but what he wanted was a night out with his wife to celebrate our individual victories and I did too but I saw it as a way to network at the same time (it was a business event!). Kev and I enjoyed our dinner, chatted to the people on our table and were having a fine time until I went to the loo and on the way back spent some of the time chatting with some of the people in the room that I knew (mostly men, so I'm told). I didn't quite realise I had spent that much time away from him (43.5mins apparently) but he got the shits (rightly so, it was my fault) and the night was ruined. We argued, it pissed us both off.

It added to the collection of unnecessary arguments we would have over the coming years, mostly fueled by alcohol.

LESSON:
Consider the other person when going out on a night out like this, the may not share your point of view. Don't argue about stupid shit anymore, it's just not worth it.

Ask Yourself:

Have you ever argued about something ridiculous that spoilt what could have been a great night out?

....

....

Do you think you could have saved the night by holding onto the straw that broke the camel's back a little longer? Remember Time and Place...

....

....

Review of life to date:
So, my 30's had been a lot tougher than my 20's but then I had added, pets, marriage, 2 kids, a business and owning property to the simple existence of my 20's. It's amazing what you can fit into 10 years. A lot of my experiences in my 30's had been great and I'm grateful for all of the incredible things I have done but I wish I would have looked back on my time and appreciated what I had more at the time, instead of spending my time feeling overwhelmed and frantic. I wish I had had the sense to ask for help.

The downward spiral

IME MOMENT:
Turning 40

Life carried on as normal for a while, work was work, the kids were growing fast. They were doing well at school, Kev's business was trucking along and mine was going well too. The day-to-day things got done, we trained, we worked, we got on with life but things weren't great at home. We were still at each other's throats. We had lost grasp of each other and quite frankly were just rubbing each other up the wrong way far too often.

The day came, and it went. I turned 40 and no new immediately identifiable wrinkles appeared (and to be honest I'm not sure I care enough about my appearance to worry about that anyway).

Kev had organised a birthday party for me at a friend of ours' café in Mooloolaba. All of our friends were there, it was a lovely party and we all had a good time. Kev had been talking to his mates on the other side of the café for a few hours and I flitted around the room trying to talk to everyone and as a consequence didn't end up drinking that much (which is remarkable for me as I'm usually first to hoe into the beer/wine/gin). The time came to go and we started to pack up, I felt like heading onto somewhere else but only Kev, Me and one other friend (who Kev was not keen on) wanted to go out. So we headed down to the surf club for a dance. I ordered drinks and gave them to Kev and my friend. She and I hit the dance floor and Kev went to the window to watch the waves crash onto the shore. I had no idea that he had drunk so much, but the fresh air must have hit him like a tonne of bricks and he faded fast...

The events of that night from that point forwards were not good. They remain as a dark shadow as another leaf of patience fell from the relationship. We left pretty quickly after I realised we really shouldn't have gone out at all (I'm not sure we even finished the 1st drink). Getting Kev home proved hard work, in fact I failed at it. After a tirade of abuse and several attempts to physically move him, I left him to suffer on his own and went home myself. He was a big boy, he was telling me to go (not quite as nicely as that) so I did. I fully expected him to get an Uber home once he'd sobered up. It never happened. At 6am I ended up searching the streets, calling the police, hospitals and all of his friends trying to find him to no avail. I went back to the place where our kids were being baby sat to wait for him and it wasn't until 10am that morning that I got a call from him telling me that he had fallen down a cliff and his phone had run out of battery. I immediately went to collect him and took him home, scowling the entire way – he was fine, just a little scratched and very hung over. Then I went back to collect the boys (there was no need for them to see their Dad like that). This is a memory that I dislike. It happened, it added to the seed of resentment I was growing inside of me and it frustrated the hell out of me.

LESSON:
Know when enough is enough, never leave anyone behind.

Ask Yourself

Are you holding onto a memory that has stained your relationship? Maybe let it go, no good will come of you holding onto it.

....

....

....

....

IME MOMENT:
Harvey dies and the fall out is tragic

In June 2016 and Harvey our Labrador had been sick for about a year. He had a tumor in his nose, it was awful to watch but as a 12-year-old lab we knew that putting him through Chemo and radiation would not prolong his life massively. It was a hard decision to make. We put him through a natural palliative care program and monitored him weekly with a local natural vet. He was given the very best care he could have asked for but as time does, it still caught up with him and took him away from us.

Our eldest Son Jake was born on the 14th June and so we needed to make sure that his birthday was not the day that Harvey went to heaven. Kev was up in Cairns doing his very first half Iron Man and when he got back, we knew it was time to stop his suffering.

I still struggle to speak about this day. Letting him go was the hardest thing I have ever done. Watching as the vet inserted the needle and then seeing his body relax knowing that his heart had stopped was so very, very distressing. As I write this I weep. It was awful, but necessary and kind. He was in so much pain, he couldn't breathe properly and his walking had deteriorated rapidly, he had had enough.

A few days after we decided to go out for a drink and try to cheer ourselves up but I guess the emotion of the past week had just overwhelmed both of us. I hid inside my shell and didn't want to face the world or anyone else's feelings – which is hard when Harvey was a family dog and we have two small boys. I acknowledge that during this week I was very selfish.

The night out ended up in yet another almighty row, where both of us showed each other our worst selves. Things were said, items were thrown and threats were made. The wedge between us just got a little deeper and that bit harder to weave back together.

Nine days after Harvey passed away and on the same day as the scattering of his ashes at the beach that he loved to play at, we went up to Diagular to choose Barry, a new addition to our family. Barry is a Bull Mastiff Rottweiler Cross. He was 6 weeks old and very cute. I thought it was too soon for a new dog, but this is the way it all panned out. The kids needed the distraction and we needed some glue to mend the broken pieces of our rapidly shattering relationship. On the 1st July we went and collected Barry and a new journey with a puppy would begin.

LESSON:
Death is hard, but life is sometimes harder when you cannot breathe. Letting someone go is more than likely the kindest thing you can do.

Ask Yourself

Are you holding onto someone or something that doesn't belong here anymore?

....

....

....

....

IME MOMENT:
Trip to France

My parents live in South West France, they moved there when Mum retired from teaching. At this time of my life I needed a break from everything. I had fallen to pieces; I had disengaged from life and felt downright fucking awful if I'm honest. My 40th year was turning to shit and it'd get worse before it got better. Kev and I knew our relationship was under the biggest test (he had no idea how fucking big this test was at that stage). I needed some breathing space. Now I'm not the kind of person to just book time away for myself, in fact I never have. Like I said earlier, Kev has always realised when I needed space and has found something for me to do and somewhere for me to go and booked it for me knowing full well that I never would. (It has something to do with my feeling of unworthiness and the mummy guilts for spending money and time on myself). Anyway, he needed a break from me and I from him, so he booked me a trip to France to hang with my Mum. He knew that something was up with me, he just had no idea what at that stage.

As I took off on the plane, I got that familiar feeling of freedom back, something that stemmed from my days as a backpacker, except this time I had a laptop (so I could still work) a suitcase on wheels (I'm shuddering at myself) and money in my pocket. Distinctly different to the days when I wore my belongings on my back like a snail and ate 2-minute noodles and bread 5 nights a week because it was filling and cheap.

My head was in a variety of different places at this stage of my life and I needed to get out of it to look at it. In hindsight, I didn't do very well with the analysis. I was in turmoil with Kev and where we were with our relationship. Work was hard work and I felt like a miserable failure who had just lost her first fur baby. Plus, stupidly - I had started something I shouldn't have with another man and I should have run for the hills, but in my current state I wasn't strong enough. I was weak and susceptible to making the biggest mistake of my life. I needed to escape to France to sort my head out. It didn't work.

Whilst in France Kev and I spoke on the phone a number of times and had big D & M's to try and sort out where we were at, but my head was in two places and he had no idea. I ended up writing him a letter telling him what I was struggling with in the relationship and he gallantly took it all on board without being objectionable.

Amidst my head fuck, I did spend a lovely 10 days with my Mum and Dad and even got to see my sisters who travelled over to hang with me for a few days too. I'd like to think that I'm close to Mum and Dad, but my sisters and I all lead such different lives that we don't connect anywhere near enough, sometimes months go by without us connecting. It's something I want to fix. The short story is that I hadn't been with my entire family for many years and so this was a very special time for me.

Mum and I were always close as I grew up into a young woman. But I was always a "Daddy's" girl as a kid and probably still am, he was always so proud of me for doing practical things, which is probably why I like being "handy" now. I was always his boy in a family of three girls. He tells this one story about me being able to climb up a ladder and fix off a beam that his workmate couldn't do, I would have been all of 11 and he was so proud. I love that story.

Anyway, I came back from France feeling less angry and much calmer but still not 100% sure of what the fuck I was doing with myself. If I could get into a time machine and go back in time I'd change so much, but mostly I'd stop what had already started to happen.

When I arrived back home in Australia, Kev and I spoke and he acknowledged my letter and said that he would change. Now I know he is capable of remarkable change because he has done it before but I did not believe him in the slightest little bit. I thought he was just saying that to manipulate the situation. I had no belief in his ability or integrity to actually change and stick to it. Perhaps in hindsight I should have given him the benefit of the doubt because he has stayed true to his word - again.

LESSON:
Take the time to think about what you want, but come back with an answer for fucks sake

Ask Yourself:

Are you in a state of disarray at the moment?
Do you have a big decision to make? Work it out before it morphs into something hideous and unchangeable.

IME MOMENT:
The mid-life crisis actually happened to me

Over the years as you can tell, my hubby and I had had our differences, he is a go-go-go kind of person and whilst I am on the go-go-go merry go round, I'm not so into the fast-paced 'lets cram it all in' lifestyle. In saying that when we are not doing something – we are bored. Go figure! We also have slightly different parenting ideas, I'm definitely more of a soft touch, but our kids have impeccable manners and extraordinary abilities because of his persistence and belief in the fact that they can do things.

We both have very different interests, not that this is a bad thing, it is just what it is, not good not bad. But what it did mean was that the time we spent together was not doing the things that both of us enjoyed together. For example, Kev really likes triathlon, the kids also like it, so I ended up getting involved but my nemesis was swimming in open water and I was kind of petrified of it, but I forced myself to do it so we could all do something together, but I ended up resenting Kev for it. I actually could have said no I'm not keen, but I didn't. Instead I made myself into a martyr and did it anyway – yay me (stupid cow). These days I still do triathlon but I'm a much better swimmer these days so it's less of an issue and who knew I'd actually enjoy it (Kev did). But it was fear that caused me to be a bitch about it. Same with surfing, Kev thought it'd be good for me to do it – to get involved so he pushed it. I was scared of the ocean. I'm over it now, but at the time it was like one challenge after the other.

See one of my problems is that I'm a people pleaser, I don't like letting people down, I have an inability to say no most of the time. I felt like I should do triathlon, because that's what he wanted, so I did. Not because I wanted to do it, so I created a ridiculous block that says that "I'm being forced to do something I don't want to do and I'm rubbish at it." So naturally I wasn't that great at it – because I've told myself I wasn't going to be great at it. Things are a little different now, as I have decided that actually I do like it, so I achieve more. Now I love going out on my bike for 4 hour rides and run and swim several times a week by choice.

When Kev was part of a rugby league footy club and he asked me if I minded if he trained them (which for a short period of the year was 4+ times a week) I'd say no, that I didn't mind, and then resent him for it, but I should have spoken up and said could it be just a few times a week as we had very young boys at that stage and I was finding it all a bit overwhelming. Instead I just built up my frustration with him and made him feel like he doing something wrong without any idea of what he was doing wrong.

Over the years the resentment grew inside of me, this seed had by now grown a stem and started to burst into flower, but I carried on being what I deemed as "normal and unobjectionable" without telling him that I was struggling. My problem was that I never really communicated how I actually felt to Kev, but would quite easily tell a friend about my qualms. Eventually Kev stopped asking me to communicate with him. I think he literally had enough of it and just got on with the things that he liked if I was not going to verbally object. (I cannot blame him, in retrospect, I was fucking hard work to live with.) As my resentment increased, the seed grew. We stopped communicating and we grew apart.

Then as described in June 2016, Harvey our Labrador died and all of my emotions came tumbling out and I'm not sure what happened from that point forwards. I think my emotional tank finally cracked. The day Harvey passed away was the worst day of my life. It shook me to my core. Harvey was our first fur baby, he was everything to me. I had such a huge bond with him that my world simply shattered. It shook Kev and the kids too but I was so self-absorbed in my own emotion I forgot about them. I've made a lot of mistakes since then.

I was sad and grieving, I'm not sure Kev really knew what to do with me. My heart literally hurt.

So, we hadn't been getting on for a while now and tensions were high. Then I did the most unthinkable and selfish thing and as eluded to; I started having an affair with a married man. If you ask me why, you know, I'm not that sure. I wanted a connection with someone I guess, I felt alone and lost. He was there at the right time and maybe he knew how to press all the right buttons. Kev reckons he read me like a book and perhaps he's right? Perhaps I went back to some of my old behaviour patterns as a teenager and then a young woman where I found that men would accept me and listen to me, so when my man wasn't listening to me, I found someone who would and who wouldn't pass judgment over whatever it was that I was doing wrong.

Starting that affair is the biggest regret of my life; I simply should not have done it. I have never felt so awful. I knew it was wrong. I knew I should stop and to be fair I did actually make this fact well known to the other man. I accept blame for it though; I cannot pass that blame onto anyone except myself. But I needed to be stronger, have more integrity and not cave in. This was probably my weakest moment as a human. I'm damaged from it.

A month or so after the affair had started, Kev had major shoulder surgery and needed me more than anything and with him was the last place I wanted to be, he knew it and so did I. I can write about this as we have now unpacked all of this. We were fractious, arguing, bitter with each other and I felt criticised at every turn (he was very critical of me, or so I felt). My head was elsewhere; I would communicate with the other man secretly when out of sight. Kev even asked me if I had met someone else – he has an amazing intuitive sense. I'm sure he felt pretty bloody awful as well if I look back, he must have felt unwanted and unloved because I was being a bitch and he knew it, as did I.

As mentioned, he had packed me off to France to go and sort my head out and escape from our tumultuous relationship for a while. I came back to a different Kev.

However, the cracks in our relationship had been there for a while and were turning into crevasses, wide enough to rip apart permanently. Even though we had spoken about salvaging our relationship and getting back to being good, I didn't believe it was possible.

Interestingly – we had had a great 6-week stint around the November of this year, the other man had gone away on an extended holiday (with his wife) and so Kev and I reconnected. Everything was going really well. Then he returned and it all fell to pieces again. I wish he had stayed away and never come back, because he returned and I went back to see him. It was dumb, it's so embarrassing and I wish I had a big eraser/blow torch for this section of my life.

I fell into the pit of despair, my depression spiralled out of control and I drank more than I'd ever drunk and combined the alcohol with Nurofen plus just to numb the pain and hide the guilt.

The other man was someone I knew from networking (which is why networking is now quite firmly NOT something I want to do). He was 15 years my senior, had adult age kids and a marriage which he described as in poor shape. We found solace in each other I guess, which sounds so ridiculous but it was what transpired. I hate myself for this. I have to let go of this so I can move forwards.

The subsequent year and a half have been more traumatic than anything I've ever experienced and I can categorically say that I never ever want to repeat it. We have argued fairly consistently since it all happened. We are still together, sometimes that feels good and sometimes I want to run as far away as I possibly can and he feels the same, but we have two small humans to think about and a life we both want to lead, so we will make it work.

I feel like I'm having a physiological response to it all. When we start to argue my heart pounds, I start to sweat, I feel like I'm shaking or vibrating inside and my response is to want to run away. I recognise this as the Flight mode. You will have heard of Fight, Flight or Freeze when it comes to dealing with highly stressful situations, well I guess I do a little bit of Fighting and a lot of the Flighting. Its something I need to stop. I'm not being chased by a tiger, it's just a disagreement.

The stress of our arguments is likely to make me sick if I'm not careful, I already know it is having a physical effect on me when arguments happen, but I don't want to develop my own disease because of avoidable stress. I need to address it. I've seen counsellors and sought advice; the funny thing is that these counsellors didn't actually tell me anything I didn't already know. They just reminded me to be patient and then asked if they could use my excel spreadsheet templates because they were good. Maybe I should be a psychologist one day!

Kev has not had it easy during this period. I literally cannot believe that I did this to us. It doesn't feel like it was me. You know I've given advice to friends in the past over the years steering them away from this sort of behaviour, yet I didn't even start to heed my own advice... In my eyes, I've failed as a human.

Working your way through a marriage breakdown is awful. It could all have been avoided if only I'd have the balls to speak up all those years ago when Kev asked me if I was ok with what he was doing instead of growing a complete fucking hedge full of resentment plants. Then building a case against him when actually I could have just been perfectly happy all along.

The affair lasted 6 months. It was not fun, actually it was hard work, living a double life with all those lies is the stupidest thing you can do, so if you are considering this – just don't. The affair consisted mostly of coffee dates, but there were some extracurricular events that took place whilst on 2 business trips out West and once in Tasmania on a trip that Kev had booked for me to go and walk in the wilderness and be alone in nature (I will never forgive myself for that one). Kev found out about the affair and two years later we are still arguing about the details and working out how we feel about the way forwards.

Most of the problem was that I drip-fed him the truth; it took nearly 6 weeks for him to finally get the truth about what went on out of me, mostly out of shame. I didn't want to divulge everything; I thought I could keep some of the detail under the rug. I hated myself for what I had done (I still do and probably always will) and felt so much guilt, shame and remorse for my actions that talking about it made it feel worse. In the end it all needed to come out so we could start to heal properly. Although he still doesn't believe me as I lied so much in the beginning – shot myself in the foot there didn't I?

I still clam up when we discuss it and it makes the heart palpitations start up again (every time). I guess I have developed anxiety and the conversation is the trigger. I'd like to think that with time I'll get over this and be able to just accept that for a period of time in my life I was the worst person could have been and I hurt the one person I've been trying to get approval from. If I can offer any advice, if you go down the road of having an affair and get caught out, admit it (everything) and then fucking move on with life in whatever way you think is best for you.

We recently decided to make a bloody good go of this fresh start we keep talking about. So, we now have date day, we now talk to each other, and we tell each other if we have issues before they become huge. We give each other space and at the same time spend time with each other. We recently decided (Kev's idea) to start again and have a go at a second marriage. That means we don't go backwards, we live life for now, not the past, we forgive each other for our past failures and we get on with being kind and loving to each other. It is possible, it's happening, sometimes it's one step forward, one step back, but mostly we are forging ahead. It's a mental journey, but one we can all do if you put your mind to it. Fuck me guys – if I can do it – you can.

We decided to move home again to give that fresh start a new abode. So, we renovated our new home, which is on an acre of space. We built a huge deck and a pool, which is beautiful – a space for us to enjoy our new "universe". We painted the walls and carpeted and tiled the floors to make it more us and we are re connecting on so many different levels, levels we have never explored before.

It's a developing relationship and it's making a difference, I'm more connected to Kev now than I have ever been in so many ways. Maybe part of my purpose on this plane is to learn how to communicate and Kev's is to learn how to forgive. Who knows? It's been the most difficult of times and I don't recommend it.

I now do things like attend Yoga Retreats and do meditation courses (encouraged by Kev as always) because I needed to find some inner calm before the physiological responses I am presenting turn themselves into something nasty and he needs me to be calmer. But I book these now. I already feel like I'm not the person I want to be anymore, I'm so far removed from the Angie that I talk about during my younger years - it's not funny. I need to get back to that free spirit, that person who knew who she was and had her head firmly attached to her shoulders and held up high. It's time. I need to let go and during these retreats and during meditation, I make major progress.

During one recent meditation, I visualised myself at a rock pool, sitting on the edge throwing rocks into the water. On these smooth black rocks was one word; these were words about things I need to remove from my life. These were Anger, Hatred, Selfishness, Not being Enough, Anxiety and Depression. I threw these rocks into the pool and watched them float down, down, down to the bottom. As they floated the words on them dissolved and the rock itself sunk into the ground never to be seen again. I actually called upon Thor to come with his hammer and smash the depression rock to dust, a neon blue hammer appeared out of the sky and smashed the rock and I swept the dust into the pool.

I don't care if you believe in Thor or not, it is all imagination and if it works then it's ok by me. They say that belief is half the cure (like the placebo effect). Then I cut some ties with some people that have affected my life. The first was Duncan, my ex from many moons ago, he dived into the pool of his own free will and never came back, not sure why he came up but he did and it was time to let that go. Then I pushed the old Kev into the water, as there were parts about him not so long ago that I didn't like, but he has done a remarkable job in changing. The last person I pushed in was the man I had an affair with. This was important, I don't want him in my life, I don't want to think about him, I want him gone, so I metaphorically drowned him so he cannot come back. I hate him and I hate what I did to my family because of my weakness, so in turn, I hate myself too. I'm learning to let that feeling go.

Then I swam in the pool with all of these transmuted emotions that had been purified. I floated around and felt great. As a result, I feel lighter, free, unbound and my worries seem to have shifted.
It's now time to heal, to get on with life and get back to being good again.

The one thing I know is that if I don't love myself, I cannot love anything else. I have to make myself better so I can give parts of myself to my loved ones who need me. My two sons, and my husband who is doing his absolute best to forgive me and move on. There are not many men out there who are this strong and for that I am grateful. We will make it work and we will live happy fulfilling lives filled with love and laughter because that is what we choose and life is a choice.

So, here's to moving forwards, here's to heeding my own bloody advice and here's to life and how good we can make it.

Ask Yourself

Have you ever done anything that you regret so deeply that it is crushing you?

....

....

Do you know how to get out of the spiral of depression that comes with these types of situations, if not seek advice?

....

....

Do you know there is help available and that meditation is one of the best things you can do to re balance yourself in times of stress?

....

Post Affair Healing

It's been fucking hard, that's my fault. I take full responsibility for the fact that I fucked up our relationship to the point where it nearly crashed and burned.

I can say that every single day since it all came to a head has been in some way shape or form tumultuous. I wake up and feel shit, I go to bed and feel shit. If we speak about it, I feel dreadful, some would argue whether it is worth it, but - it is.

As two humans who have been through 16 years of life journeying together, we have a lot to hold onto. Every relationship has it's ups and downs. We have just been through the biggest down, so now its time for some UP!

Once you've been to the bottom the only way is up right? I'm sure as hell not staying laying lifeless on the bottom any longer. Fuck that!

Part of the process of healing has involved, much to my disgust – talking about it, in detail. It makes me shudder, but Kev now knows about everything. Every detail I hate myself for is on the table.

I've accepted that Kev has actually changed for the better, because I asked him to and now I need to change for him – for the better to make this work. I've had to decide to consciously change who I am. I am (hopefully) now more considerate of him; I pay more attention to his needs (and he mine).

I've had to try not to get so angry when we "talk", to not fly off the handle at his desire to "question" me. Its all part of his healing process (but by God its difficult) because guilt and self-loathing take over and consume me (sometimes for days).

We do more things together, including exercise, we intentionally spend days together doing things we like. It's a process of falling back in love with each other and it seems to be working. I think there are times when we both "pretend" but most of the time we are actually being authentic – we have to if this is to survive.

I think I need to realise that I have someone on my side. He's not working against me, he's there for me - obviously - through thick and thin. For that I commend him, he is rare and to be treasured. I need to potentially pull my head out of my arse and stop feeling like he's coercing me into doing stuff, he's trying to enhance my life and make me live my dreams. He takes us travelling (because I like travelling) He encourages me to write (so he built me a desk), paint (so he bought me an easel and paints), play the guitar (so he bought me a guitar), meditate (So he bought me a meditation cushion, rug and candles), I've always wanted a motorbike (so he found one and we bought it) – actually it's very cool, it's a 1967 Yamaha 100. So, he has always been on my side. He is very good at spending money on me and thinking about me. I'm crap at it.

In return I've stopped making him feel like he shouldn't train (I didn't know I did this – but apparently I did make him feel like he couldn't). I'll do things like make his lunch (he likes it), we catch up during the day for coffee at times, I'll buy him little things occasionally to show him I love him. I now try and book trips myself for all of us to go on, it's always been him that does it all. I've even tried to be a tad more interesting in the bedroom and initiate sex (not my strong point, but it needs to be part of our way forwards). We are both making an effort.

We agreed to stop fighting. One of things we have done is to both get a porcupine tattooed on our wrists, it's no ordinary porcupine, I drew this one, it's a line drawing, and our porcupine has a feathered tail, so our prickles turn to something softer. It's a permanent reminder etched into our skin to be kinder to each other. It works, we often call "porcupine" if arguments are getting nowhere and are just at stalemate.

Another thing we have gotten better at is being on the same page in regards to parenting. Sometimes we would be like chalk and cheese and end up confusing the kids with our varied responses. Now we talk about the issue, decide upon a solution and then together we respond to the kids backing each other up and making the environment and instruction easier for the kids to understand.

If you are at odds with your partner and your parenting styles, you need to address this. It's not the children's' fault that you have different values or ideas of how situations should be handled. But you need to find a way to collectively solve a problem without confusing your child. Our kids learn from us and they will likely just repeat our mistakes in their adult lives if we do not unite on our life message to them. As parents, we are here to guide our kids not be best mates with them, so we are now much better at this. It's a huge weight off of my shoulders.

Look, there are days when we still rub each other up the wrong way, but essentially, we are back "there" for each other.
It's not easy, but it is possible.

Summary:
This idea came to me whilst cooling down after the long hot sweaty hill running session. I knew it wasn't me dreaming this stuff up, this was one of those moments where an idea or a concept attaches itself to you so you can bear the fruit from its innocent seed. Like I described in the chapter that mentions the book "Big Magic".
So the seed said, "You no longer have a master, you are your own master, this is why you have changed".

I thought about it. It is true. Lately I have changed, I'm no longer who I was, they say that all of the cells in your body completely renew every 7 years, so I'm actually not who I was both emotionally and physically. This idea initially came about after a soul cleansing healing I had in August

2016. In this session I did an akashic record review and I had a binding from a previous life that was attached to me - removed. It was a binding that had made me feel like I was being persecuted for being who I wanted to be. After a 21-day process this binding was lifted and remarkably things started to alter in my perception and as a consequence, my world.

I've always been the kind of person, who needs to have some sort of approval from someone in some way shape or form, but I seem to have let go of this rather annoying trait and I'm running my own race now. Part of my make up over the past 42 years has been to seek approval from leaders or teachers around me. These people included my parents, teachers, employers, people I looked up to, my clients, my staff, my husband, everyone. Then I got bored as it began to suffocate me, to bring me down and it made me feel heavy. After the cleansing I've been trying hard to let it go. It's by no means an easy task, but when my akashic records were changed, I changed.

Whether it is fact or has any iota of truth makes not one dot of difference to me. I don't care if you believe in a goldfish god or that we are all just here to live then die. If you can inherently change something in your make up that is holding you back by altering your belief or the way you feel and then respond to a situation differently, more positively, then it is whatever it is and I'm ok with that.

Another thought then crossed my mind whilst I cooled down and let the warm Queensland sun beat down on my red face. Yet again, it wasn't me, I was being told this.

"All your soul desires is happiness, so be happy."

Your vibration attracts similar vibrations, so if you are near someone who is sad or angry, you will soon start to be sad or angry too because like sound waves, vibrations are energy and they affect the environment we live in and the beings that reside in that space. Similarly, if you are upset or blue, you will gift that emotion to the people you are with or to whom you are connected and it brings everyone down. So, in order to find that happiness your soul is yearning for, it's simple. All you have to do is be happy. Vibrate on a happy level, let go of the daily struggle, find the gold in every situation."

There is a school of thought that we are here to learn lessons. I buy into this theory. Imagine Earth being like one of those physical skill-based obstacle course shows that has a variety of different challenges and you have to work your way though the series of increasingly difficult tasks. Well, life is like that. Sometimes you are going to get smacked in the face with a big red plastic pole and sometimes you'll fall off into the deep dark waters below, but the challenge is to get back up, to keep on trying and to have fun doing it.

So, if Earth is our school, and our uniform is our human skeleton and flesh (no matter what colour or shape), shouldn't we all be working towards completing the tasks in the funniest, happiest, most amusing way ever? Instead of giving up and thinking that everything is too hard, of course it's hard, it's a lesson.

So, next time you are feeling like giving up and you are feeding off of the vibration of someone around you - do these things.

- Put yourself into a bubble of protection, I don't care how you do this; just think happy thoughts and the anger will subside

- Improve your own vibration by doing something you love, walking, reading, listening to music, dancing, whatever it is. Side note: I'd suggest that whatever it is, it involves putting aside the technological distractions and getting back to being you without the temptation of hiding behind a screen and faking your existence.

- Do something nice for someone else, because there is beauty and happiness in giving and paying it forward. It'll make you feel so much better and turn that frown upside down.

Consider this: You are right where you are supposed to be and that you are going through your series of challenges in this life as you for a reason – what is the reason, what is the ultimate truth that you will derive from these situations?

Before you were born, there is a theory that you set up this life so you had to learn a few key lessons. It might be that your soul needs to learn more patience and so you are put into situations that make you impatient, to test you. It might be that you need to learn how to forgive and so you are thrust into life challenges where you are treated badly so you can at some point work towards being able to forgive those who hurt you. It's amazing to think of life like this, but it might help you to make sense of why your life has taken the particular path it has.

So again, I note that if the soul wants to learn these lessons and just be happy, then learn them, stop resisting and live the happiest, best life you can with the tools you have been given because next time round you'll have a whole different set of challenges and you'll need to have built up your resilience to face those ones head on too.

What's next?

So, I've unpacked my life to date. I learnt a heap about myself in the process. Ask yourself if you had any "aha" moments during your short read. Did you answer the questions? I hope you did, I hope you wrote down some notes and that you start to look at the world through slightly different lenses as a result.

Read your answers, note down the ones that require further attention – then get off of your backside and do something about it. It's your life.

De-clutter
Now what to do with all this amazing insight?
I guess if you've started to analyse the piles of junk you've accumulated over the course of your life you cannot just leave these piles out there to fester, you kind of have to package them up into sections. Then you need to either store them for future use in an orderly manner or dare I say it – let them go.

So for me, this book was all about me working out why I am the way I am, why I have these behaviours, what I've learnt and what I need to retain from life so far. It has taught me that whilst this is my life, I'm not the only one in it. Its illustrated to me that I am not better than anyone else, in fact right now I feel like I'm less, but that feeling will eventually subside. But probably the most important thing I've learnt is that I have learnt the lesson and now, its simply time to let go of the memory and the binding that ties me to that moment in time.

Therefore out goes the memory that I was bullied, out goes the hate that I felt for those girls. I'm letting go of the fact that I never really felt like I fit in, because I didn't and the fact is, I didn't want to either, so holding onto the anger of not being in the popular group and needing constant approval from other humans is really debilitating and in all honestly in hindsight – stupid, because I never wanted it anyway, so I choose to let it go and let it stop holding me back. Out goes the fear I had from an old relationship and out goes the panic I have when I argue with my husband – I'm not being hunted down. As far as I can throw, I choose to banish all thoughts of guilt, hate and betrayal from my sphere of influence, that time is over. I no longer choose to have depression, I choose to be happy and hold my head high. We all make mistakes, we all have emotions we cannot fathom, but we are all still amazing humans and we should all still love ourselves regardless.

I choose to be me, the real authentic me, the one that likes to be alone, the one that likes to push the boundaries, the one that is creative, sarcastic, smart, passionate, musical, interested, spiritual, inspirational, yet sometimes quiet, silent, alone (but not lonely), absorbed and peaceful.

Do you know what? I like who I am! It's taken me a long time to realise that I'm ok. I'm 42 and I'm enough, I'm good at what I do, I like what I do, I like who I am (now) and the journey that I have taken to sculpt this. The Angie that is typing this isn't always happy, she thinks too much, is sometimes scared shitless, analyses too much, and at times, still doesn't believe in herself – but, I'm human, I'm a work in progress and right now, I'm enough, I'm adequate.

I'm finally chucking out all the ridiculous baggage I've carried around the world (literally) and making space for new amazing creative experiences to take place. Who knows what's around the corner, all I know is that I'm as prepared as I can be for the next big chapter of my life. I'll always unpack a little more and make space for the new, its cathartic and necessary. I'm not after a round of applause or anyone's opinion from this book, but I know that some people I know might think less of me because of my more recent mistakes. All I can say is that everyone is entitled to his or her opinion. I just don't have to hold onto their opinion like a torch and let it consume me. So, I won't.

Maybe it's time that you did a little de-cluttering too. It's simply impossible to keep on do, do, doing and keep on filling and taking and building. At some point you'll crack, so instead of waiting for the giant crevasse to appear, take charge of your life, get rid of the burdens and those feelings that don't serve you. Consider replacing them with lighter, more fun filled, authentic things that you love. Its time to take out the rubbish that you've been storing in your pockets all this time. This is your journey, not your partners, not your kids, not your parents, not anyone else's – it's yours. Don't worry so much about other people's opinions about what you do – who fucking cares what they think. Go fill your gaps with creativity, spontaneity, laughter, and fun and start enjoying you and your life again.

What is it that you are looking for in this life now?

I love my life and how it has all unfolded, even the most painful parts because I have learnt more about who I am as a result of what I have experienced. (It's actually hard to say that as it has been so hard over the past few years). The fabric of my life is rich and strong, woven from varying threads from various balls of yarn from all over the globe all tightly knitted together. At some point, as I have illustrated the pattern and the overall picture starts to emerge on your tapestry and you can stand back and admire your work of art - you.

Go and weave yourself a life worth unpacking and tell me about your adventures and what you've learnt along the way.

Wipe your feet on the way out...

Need to be unpacked?

Angie is available to speak topics such as:

- Human Behaviour (from her perspective, not a textbook - she is not a psychologist)
- Running a Business, being a Mum, being a wife, being everything and still surviving with your identity intact.
- Why being fit has changed me from the inside out - healthy body, happy life.
- How to unpack your life and get on with just being enough
- Why understanding and impregnating your values into your business is critical to your business success

Angie also provides mentoring services to businesses across the globe that have people and marketing problems. Driving business change is what Angie does best.. Contact her to unpack both you, your staff and your business so she can re pack you and help your business and life to change for the better.

- Mentoring you
- Mentoring business

Disclaimer:
Angie is not a life coach, doctor, psychologist or professional in any way shape or form - she just uses common sense to clarify obvious issues and using her blunt edge she can help you to see a better path. Angie does not sugar coat, be prepared to be unpacked.
See **unpacking.com.au** for more details.

www.ingramcontent.com/pod-product-compliance
Lightning Source LLC
Chambersburg PA
CBHW071924290426
44110CB00013B/1470